COMPLETE GUIDE
FOR HAVING
CHILDREN
WITH
PERFECT TEETH

An easy-to-follow Guide for Future Parents,
Parents, Nurses, Dentists, and Physicians,
providing all the information needed.

Providing Proven Information: the Most
Important of which has been kept from the
Public for over 45 years by Dental Organizations
protecting the Income of Dentists.

FRANCES B. GLENN, DDS
WILLIAM D. GLENN, III, MD

Bloomington, IN 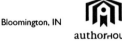 Milton Keynes, UK

authorHOUSE®

AuthorHouse™
1663 Liberty Drive, Suite 200
Bloomington, IN 47403
www.authorhouse.com
Phone: 1-800-839-8640

AuthorHouse™ UK Ltd.
500 Avebury Boulevard
Central Milton Keynes, MK9 2BE
www.authorhouse.co.uk
Phone: 08001974150

First published by AuthorHouse   5/2/2007

ISBN: 978-1-4259-8430-4 (e)
ISBN: 978-1-4259-8427-4 (sc)
ISBN: 978-1-4259-8431-1 (hc)

Library of Congress Control Number: 2006911249

Printed in the United States of America
Bloomington, Indiana

This book is printed on acid-free paper.

WHAT THE EXPERTS SAY

"I agree with and support Dr. Glenn's findings and her program."

Dr. Itzak Gedalia, Ph.D., Professor, Hebrew-Hadassah Dental School. Israel's and Europe's most accomplished dental researcher. Jerusalem, Israel

"I prescribed Dr. Glenn's recommendations for my patients."

Dr. Charles Kalstone, M.D., Named "Miami's Obstetrician To The Stars." Miami, Florida

"Dr. Glenn's book should be read by everyone concerned with children's health."

Dr. Herbert Scharpf, D.M.D., Captain, US Navy Dental Corp, (Ret.), Former Chief of Oral & Maxillofacial Surgery, US Navy Hospital, San Diego, California

"This book offers abundant information about dental health that is not generally available to the public and 'tells it like it is'".

Dr. Benedict Homer, D.D.S., Past President, American Orthodontic Society, Dallas, Texas

ABOUT THE BOOK

The book gives future parents, parents, nurses, dentists, and physicians simple, proven, step-by-step directions for producing children whose teeth will not have cavities, can be protected from injury, and can often avoid the need for straightening. If orthodontics is required, you learn how to obtain the best results at the most reasonable cost. On another level, you learn how private dental organizations have managed to keep the knowledge of cavity-free children from the public for over 45 years.

OTHER BOOKS BY THE AUTHORS

How to Have Children with Perfect Teeth © 2000, 380 pages. Published by The Children's Dental Research Society, Inc.

OTHER PUBLICATIONS BY THE AUTHORS

The authors have published 19 research papers in peer-reviewed medical and dental journals, including *Journal of Dentistry for Children, Journal of Dental Research,* and *American Journal of Obstetrics and Gynecology.* The papers that are especially relevant to this book are listed in the appendix.

DEDICATION

The authors dedicate this book to our parents, teachers, professors, and mentors who formed, helped, and guided us along our path; to the pioneers in preventive nutrition who preceded us and whose work we reference in our published papers; to the true scientists named in our papers who aided in our research; to the two generations of parents, over 3,000 of them, who understood what we were doing and allowed us to help them produce children with "perfect teeth;" and finally and perhaps most importantly, to the late George Teuscher, D.D.S., Ph.D., whose towering intellect and uncompromising integrity were universally recognized during his 65 year dental career—highlighted by his 19 years as Dean of Northwestern University's School of Dentistry, and his 32 years as Editor of *the Journal of Dentistry for Children*. Without his support, this book probably could not have been written.

2007 DEDICATION

We should also remember the 140 million children who have suffered unnecessary dental disease in the past 45 years, especially those whose tooth cavities resulted in permanent injury or death. Ten years ago, one hospital in Florida, Broward General, admitted two nine year olds, in just one year, whose decayed baby molars had led to face and brain infection. Heroic treatment saved their lives, but both were left with permanent brain damage. In the 1980s, Denver General Hospital had, in just one year, three young children die from anesthetic mishaps while getting their teeth repaired. (Hospital anesthesia for children is safer now.) In September 2006, 5 year old Diamond Brownridge died in Chicago from dental office sedation needed to repair her ravaged teeth with caps. The American Dental Association and the Academy of Pediatric Dentistry told reporters that thay had no statistics on how often this occurs. They pretend they don't know anything about it as they want the subject to disappear from the news as soon as possible.

Quiz for Readers: Test Your Dental & Political Knowledge

Facts: Almost 50 years ago, Drs. Dietz and Beuhl, of St. Louis, MO, and Dr. Feltman, of Passaic, NJ published that they had produced children's teeth that were immune to decay. Since then, there have been 14 more confirming trials and reports published in the dental literature.

Question: Why now is tooth decay still the most common chronic disease of children and is second only to colds and flues as the most common acute illness of childhood?

Answers: Find the <u>one</u> that is incorrect.

1. The American Dental Association (ADA) protecting dentists' incomes.
2. Government Agencies that are supposed to help children are controlled by lobbyists working for the ADA.
3. Teeth are the only organ not controlled by physicians.
4. Vice-President Dick Cheney's false teeth.
5. Subversion of the Centers for Disease Control by a foreign-based cult.

How did you do? Never mind, when you read this book, you will know all this and more.

FUNDING

We are most grateful to the Walter G. Ross Foundation, Washington, DC, and to the Children's Dental Research Society, Vero Beach, FL and Washington, DC, for funding our research. This book is published by the Children's Dental Research Society, a US Treasury Department approved tax-free charitable organization, and the proceeds from the sale of this book go to the Society for the benefit of children.

The Children's Dental Research Society
is a long time Institutional Member of the
American Association for Dental Research
and the
International Association for Dental Research
headquartered in Alexandria, VA

Drawings
by the late
William Bodenhamer,
Miami, FL

ACKNOWLEDGMENTS

For invaluable help in our research the authors thank Dr. Robert Fitzgerald, the Veterans Administration Hospital; Dr. Racquel LeGeros, New York University Dental School; Dr. Dosuk Lee, Harvard Medical School Bone Research Lab, Children's Hospital; Dr. Irving Shapiro, University of Pennsylvania Dental School; Dr. Andrew Shillen, University of South Africa; Dr. Alphonse Burdi, University of Michigan Medical School; the late Dr. William Lyons, American Dental Association Lab; and the late Dr. Leon Singer, University of Minnesota Medical School.

We also wish to thank the late Patrick Stocker, Dental Promotions Limited, London; Professor Picton, University of London Dental School; the late Dr. Michel Serfaty, Paris; Dr. Francine Serfaty-Ziza, Paris; Dr. Monique Schouker Jolly, Paris; and a special thanks to Dr. Michel Schouker, founder of the World Congress of Preventive Dentistry, also of Paris.

For informing us about the mishandling of folic acid in pregnancy by nutritionists and obstetricians in the 1970s and 1980s, we thank Dr. Lynn B. Bailey, Professor of Nutrition, University of Florida.

About the author, *Frances B. Glenn, D.D.S.*

EDUCATION AND EXPERIENCE:

- Attended public schools in Tampa, Florida, graduating in January 1951.

- Attended University of Florida and entered University of Pennsylvania School of Dental Medicine in 1952, graduating in 1956.

- Trained in Children's Dentistry at Children's Hospital, Washington, D.C., and spent one day a week at the National Institute of Dental Research at the Institutes of Health (NIH) where her interest in research, which began at the University of Pennsylvania, was encouraged, 1956-1957.

- Private practice of Pediatric Dentistry, near Eglin Air Force Base, Florida, 1957-1959.

- Private practice of Pediatric Dentistry and Pediatric Orthodontics, South Miami, Florida from 1959 to 2001.

AFFILIATIONS / ACCOMPLISHMENTS:

- American Society of Dentistry for Children

- American Academy of Pediatric Dentistry

- Children's Dental Research Society

- American Orthodontic Society

- Fellow, American Academy of Pediatric Dentistry since 1964.

- Who's Who in American Women, 1964

- Trained in straight wire orthodontics under the auspices of the Straight Wire Foundation at the clinics of Louisiana State University Dental School, 1977-1979.

- Diplomate of the Board of the American Orthodontic Society, 1982.

- First woman dentist to receive the Outstanding Alumni Award, University of Pennsylvania School of Dental Medicine, 1984.

- Member, Board of Overseers, University of Pennsylvania School of Dental Medicine, 1990 to present.

- First woman dentist to receive the Dr. Richard L. Moore Distinguished Service Award by the American Orthodontic Society, 1994.

- Who's Who in American Medicine and Health Care, 1999

- Guide to America's Top Dentists, 2000, by the Consumers Research Council of America.

- Her research in the fields of Congenitally Missing Teeth and Fluoride Nutrition has been published in numerous national medical and dental journals and has been cited in many medical and dental texts including the *Yearbook of Dentistry*, 1979-1980; Sciarra's *Obstetrics and Gynecology*, 1980-1988; Danforth, 4th Edition, *Obstetrics and Gynecology*, 1982; Shapiro, *Obstetrics and Gynecology*, 1983; *Pediatric Dentistry*, Stuart, 1983; *Dental Clinics of North America*, 1984; and *Dietary Reference Intakes for Calcium, Phosphorus, Magnesium, Vitamin D, and Fluoride, National Academy of Sciences, Washington, D.C., 1997.*

LECTURES:

- University of Miami School of Medicine

- Miami Dade School of Dental Hygiene

- Florida International University

- The American Dental Association Annual Meeting

- The American Academy of Pediatric Dentistry

- University of London College of Dentistry

- University of Paris Dental School

- The American Association for Dental Research

- The International Association for Dental Research

- The University of Texas School of Medicine

- University of Colorado School of Medicine

- The World Congress of Preventive Dentistry, Paris, France, 1987 and Fukuoka, Japan, 1991.

- And others.

About the co-author, *W. Darby Glenn, III, M.D.*

EDUCATION:

- Attended and graduated from public school in Tenafly, New Jersey, 1949.

- Harvard University, A.B., 1952 (cl '53).

- University of Pennsylvania Medical School, M.D., 1956.

- Internship, Walter Reed Army Hospital, Washington, D.C., 1956-1957.

- General Medical Officer, United States Air Force, Eglin Air Force Base, Florida, 1957-1959.

- Resident, University of Miami School of Medicine, 1959- 1962 in Otolaryngology (Ear, Nose & Throat), and Head and Neck Surgery.

AFFILIATIONS / ACCOMPLISHMENTS:

- Diplomate, American Board of Otolaryngology, Head and Neck Surgery, 1963.

- Instructor and Assistant Clinical Professor, Otolaryngology and Head and Neck Surgery, University of Miami School of Medicine, 1962-1975.

- Private Practice Otolaryngology, Head and Neck Surgery, South Miami, Florida, 1962-2001.

- Consultant to the Florida Board of Medical Examiners in Tallahassee, Florida, 1990-2003.

- Member Dade County Medical Association, 1962-2001.

- Member Florida Medical Association, 1962-2001.

- Member American Medical Association, 1962-2001.

- Member Indian River County Medical Society, 2003-present.

- American Association for Dental Research

- International Association for Dental Research

- Fellow, American Academy of Otolaryngology, Head and Neck Surgery.

- Assisted his wife, Frances, in her Fluoride Nutrition Research and her lectures, and is co-author of some of her publications, 1981-present.

CHILDREN
with
PERFECT TEETH

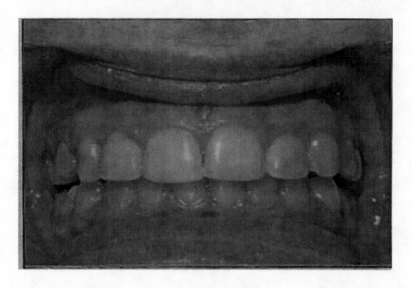

WHAT DO WE MEAN BY "PERFECT TEETH"?

1. Teeth with such quality enamel and relatively smooth chewing surfaces that they will not have any cavities.

2. Teeth that are protected from injury or trauma.

3. Straight teeth that mesh well together for proper chewing and that look good.

4. Healthy gums and jawbones around these teeth.

THESE ARE OUR GOALS

The first goal—cavity free children—is the easiest and the cheapest—for about $20 a year per child anyone can have children whose teeth will have maximum resistance to decay. The other goals require help from a dentist, so we will tell you how to choose a dentist and how to make certain your dentist is doing quality dentistry at a reasonable cost.

Table of Contents

QUESTIONS AND ANSWERS

Q. Everyone in our family has soft teeth that decay easily. Can you change that?

A. We can change that easily, safely, and cheaply—unless you think $20.00 a year is expensive (plus the cost of this book!).

Q. I know that if children eat no sweets and brush every time they eat, their teeth will be pretty good—so is the secret of cavity free children just more of that sort of advice?

A. No. We call that a "eat more broccoli and brush 12 times a day book." There is nothing wrong with the advice except that it is impractical and not in tune with the real world of children. We think that occasionally eating an Oreo™ is a part of childhood and we want our children's teeth to be able to withstand a normal American diet.

Q. If I read this book, will I learn something I don't already know?

A. You will learn many things you don't already know and you will learn things that your dentist and certainly your physician don't know.

Q. How much money can I save by reading this book and following its instructions?

A. Thousands of dollars can be saved. Teeth that are especially resistant to decay are worth many thousands of dollars in saving over the life of each of your children. Actually, the value of having quality teeth that don't decay cannot be stated in terms of money. In addition, the section on orthodontics alone can save several thousand dollars and have your kids end up with better smiles.

Q. If the kids' teeth are going to be so good, why are there chapters on diet?

A. Children's diet matters because it affects the overall health of the child.

Q. Is this some new experimental thing?

A. No, it was first suggested by an English physician in 1892 as a solution to the terrible condition of British teeth. He was ignored and the English still have the worst teeth in the industrialized world. It was first used in the US with total success in the 1950s.

Q. Why doesn't my doctor know about it?

A. It was squelched, first by the National Institute of Dental Research at NIH for fear it would interfere with water fluoridation. Later, dental organizations protecting the incomes of their members joined in. They were aided by Dental School Professors working for the toothpaste and sealant industry.

Q. How could they get away with doing that?

A. Very easily, thanks to politics and the Golden Rule.

Q.	You mean do unto others what you would have them do unto you?

A.	No, we mean those who send the most gold to Washington DC, rule.

Q.	And that harms children?

A.	The money that the Dental Lobby supplies Congressmen and Senators gives dental organizations control of dental matters in the Government Agencies that are supposed to look after our children's best interest. That is why tooth decay is still the most common chronic disease in children and is the second most common acute disease in children. (Respiratory illnesses, colds, and flues are first). This is almost 50 years after doctors in St. Louis, Missouri and Passaic, New Jersey demonstrated that children can have teeth that do not decay.

SECTION I
CAVITY FREE CHILDREN

SECTION I

CAVITY FREE CHILDREN

How to have children whose teeth do not decay—children who will not have cavities and therefore will not need fillings, and who usually do not have to have temporary plastic surface fillings (sealants) placed by the dentist. This section is put first in the book—before the chapter on how to choose a dentist for your child, because the quality of most of your children's teeth will have already been decided by the time of the first visit to that dentist at about age 3 years.

CRITICALLY IMPORTANT CONCEPT

The features of your child's teeth that provide maximum cavity prevention—hard white dense outer enamel for all the teeth and relatively smooth chewing surfaces for the molars have already been determined for the primary teeth (baby teeth, milk teeth) and for the first permanent molars (six year molars) at birth, and have already been determined for most of the rest of the permanent teeth, except for the wisdom teeth, by age 3 years. The teeth are a done deal before your child ever sees a dentist! So it is up to you, but don't get nervous, it is easy.

CHAPTER ONE

THE SECRET OF CAVITY FREE TEETH

One hundred years ago, children were often born with soft bones due to a lack of calcium and vitamin D in their mother's diet. When these children started to walk, their bones would bend and they would be diagnosed as having rickets. This mineral deficiency disease is now prevented by supplying the mother-to-be and the child with enough calcium in their diet and in their calcium-vitamin supplements.

There is a mineral which is just as essential for forming quality enamel in teeth as calcium is for forming quality bones, and the secret of having cavity free teeth is to provide the correct amount of this tooth mineral while the child's teeth are forming. The name of this essential tooth mineral is **fluoride.**

"Fluoride," you say, "I already know about it—we use it in our toothpaste and I think it is put in our water supply or our children take it with their vitamins—what is so secret about fluoride?" **The secret is in providing fluoride in the ideal amount during the <u>entire time</u> the teeth are forming.** The reason why this is so important is that once tooth enamel is formed it cannot be changed. Bones are somewhat different. If not enough calcium is given during early bone formation, it can be given later and it will then be built into the bones which are constantly being broken down and reforming, as are most of the tissues and organs in our body. Tooth enamel behaves more like hair and fingernails; once formed, there is little or no active metabolism or change in the cells. In addition, the amount of fluoride present at the start of tooth development determines how much fluoride can be built into the tooth enamel during the final stage of development one to nine years later! What you first make in the way of tooth enamel is what you end up with, and it is the amount

5

of fluoride built into the tooth enamel that primarily determines how resistant the tooth is to cavities.

The way in which fluoride is now used is designed to give a 50-60 percent reduction in children's cavities. The way in which we instruct you to give fluoride results in a 99 percent reduction in children's cavities, which means that 98 percent of the children will probably never have a cavity or have a filling, and 95 percent will not need temporary plastic coatings (sealants) which can develop hidden leaks and allow large cavities to form undetected.

What do you need to do that is not generally being done now? In a nutshell, you must take fluoride tablets in pregnancy, which is when the primary teeth (baby teeth) and the six-year molars (first permanent molars) are forming, and you must supplement the baby and the child with fluoride drops and tablets even if you live in a community that puts fluoride in its water supply (fluoridated water), because that is when the rest of the permanent teeth start developing.

Q. Must I read and understand all of the scientific material in order to have children with no cavities?

A. No, you can just follow the dosage tables in Chapter 2 however, anyone who can read can understand the material in this book and we think it is important for parents to understand what to do so that they can take charge of a prevention program. No one is more interested in the quality of your child's teeth than you are.

Q   Isn't it dangerous to take medicine or drugs in pregnancy?

A   Fluoride is not medicine or a drug, it is a natural mineral element recognized as an essential nutrient by the Food and Nutrition Board of the American Academy of Sciences, Washington, D.C. in 1968, and by the Food and Drug Administration in 1973. In 1999, this US official Food and Nutrition Board determined that pregnant women need a minimum of 3 milligrams (mg) of fluoride a day. As your diet and water gives you 0.5-2 mg a day, if you do not take a fluoride supplement while pregnant, you and the fetus have a nutritional deficiency. It is actually dangerous not to take fluoride in pregnancy, as if you do not, the child's teeth may be especially soft and the child may require a strong sedative or even general anesthesia in order to repair these teeth at a very early age, which always involves some risk.

Q.   I am one of the 55 percent of Americans who live in a community with fluoridated water. My physician and/or dentist told me that we get all the fluoride we need in the water.

A   It was shown in the 1960s that almost all the fluoride in fluoridated water that a pregnant woman drinks is excreted in her urine and absorbed by her bones before it can reach the teeth forming in the fetus (unborn child). Fluoridation of your water was designed to be drunk by children, mostly for their permanent teeth. No one ever claimed that fluoridated water provided enough fluoride for the fetal teeth during pregnancy; instead, the need for pregnancy fluoride was ignored. Dentists did not feel comfortable dealing with pregnant women and dental organizations were and are still terrified that physicians will take over dental prevention. Most obstetricians do not regard the quality of the children's teeth as their responsibility and only know about fluoride what they are told by dentists, and therefore fluoride supplementation in pregnancy has fallen between the cracks (pushed by the dental lobby, actually).

As for fluoridated water for children, the amount of fluoride in fluoridated water was set by a study done in 1940, using 12 to 14 year old children in rural communities who had grown up during the great economic depression of the 1930s. Children drank more water in those days because their families could not afford other beverages and the amount of fluoride in the water was picked so that no matter how much water a child drank, no child would get an excessive amount of fluoride. Therefore, the amount of fluoride in fluoridated water is too low and the intake of water too variable from one day to the next for any child to get the correct daily amount in order to perfect their teeth. All municipal water systems should be fluoridated as it provides some fluoride for all children and improves their teeth approximately 50 to 60 percent, but we can do better for each individual child. Therefore, most children need to be supplemented with fluoride in infancy and childhood amount using the schedules provided in this book. This is especially critical in the southern parts of the United States which are fluoridated with little more than half the of fluoride originally picked in 1940 as ideal for a community.

Q   I already have children, so I cannot start fluoride in pregnancy. Is it too late?

A.   It is never too late to improve your children's teeth with the use of supplemental fluoride. It may be too late to perfect their teeth, but you should give fluoride if teeth are still forming, which is to age 12 or 13 for the regular permanent teeth and until age 18 to 21 for the wisdom teeth, as well as for some benefit to the bone around the teeth and possibly for strengthening all the bones in the body.

Fluoride is for teeth what calcium is for bones.

My mom didn't take fluoride during my pregnancy and when I eat and drink, my teeth melt.

My mom didn't take calcium during my pregnancy and when I walked, my legs bent.

Picture of authors with President G.H.W. Bush.

He has one prenatal fluoride supplemented grandchild.

Picture of Dr. Frances Glenn with Congressman Sam Gibbons (Democrat, Florida), then Chairman of the Ways and Means Committee.

He has two prenatal fluoride supplemented grandchildren. Preventive nutrition knows no political boundaries!

CHAPTER TWO

FLUORIDE SUPPLEMENT DOSAGE FOR PREGNANCY AND FOR INFANTS AND CHILDREN

IN PREGNANCY

For pregnant women, the dosage of fluoride is very simple. This is because there is a lot of leeway and, therefore, it does not matter if the water is fluoridated or not. All the fluoride a pregnant woman ingests is immediately diluted in about 40 liters (9 gallons) of her body fluids and most of the fluoride is excreted in her urine, or taken up by her bones. By taking fluoride tablets on an empty stomach, the fluoride level in the mother-to-be's blood rises for about an hour and a little fluoride gets to the fetus and it is built into the enamel that is forming in all the primary teeth (baby teeth) and the six-year molars (first permanent molars). We will show you later how this built-in fluoride greatly improves the quality of teeth. Ninety-nine percent of women in this country live either in a non-fluoridated, fluoride-deficient area or in a fluoridated area. These areas, which include all of our large cities and suburbs, will have less than two parts per million (ppm) of fluoride in the water. Most have 0.1 to 1.0 ppm. You can find out from your water company or your Public Health Department, as you will need to know for supplementing young children, but for pregnancy, it does not matter. All women in these areas should take 2 milligrams (mg) of fluoride, which is two tablets, each containing 1-milligram (mg) of fluoride, a day on an empty stomach, not followed by a meal, especially a calcium meal such as milk or cheese, for 30 minutes to 1 hour. Take the two tablets together, daily, starting about the 12th week of pregnancy, and continue until delivery. Take your vitamin-mineral pregnancy capsule at a different time of day since it contains calcium that can bind with the fluoride in the stomach and makes the fluoride less bio-available if taken at the same time as the calcium. When a 2 mg or even a 3 mg fluoride tablet becomes available, one of those a day will do nicely.

Less than 1 percent of the population lives in high fluoride areas. These are mostly west of the Mississippi River; Oklahoma, Colorado, and West Texas. The Food and Nutrition Board of the National Academy of Sciences designates 3 mg of fluoride a day as the minimum for pregnant women and 10 mg a day as the maximum. Therefore, 99 percent of the women in this country, which includes all the major cities and suburbs, need to take two fluoride tablets a day during their pregnancy in order to try to perfect their children's teeth by getting at least the minimum fluoride needed.

The twelfth week of pregnancy is approximately one week after the date that your third missed period would have started. The first missed period means you are about two weeks pregnant. The second missed period makes you about six weeks pregnant and the third missed period date is about the $10^{th} - 11^{th}$ week of pregnancy. This is about when the primary (baby) teeth start to form. For trying to perfect the six-year (first permanent) molars, it is necessary to start by the fifth month of pregnancy. So, no matter where you are now in pregnancy, start it. But, if you want to try to perfect all the teeth, you must start by the twelfth week. You can start the fluoride before the twelfth week or even before the pregnancy begins if you like, but it is not absolutely needed until the teeth begin to mineralize about the twelfth week.

Pregnancy Supplement of Fluoride Tablets

Amount of fluoride in the water	12th week of pregnancy to term
It does not matter how much fluoride is in the water for 99% of the women in the USA	2 mg fluoride (2 tablets of 2.2 mg sodium fluoride) a day taken on an empty stomach and not followed by a calcium supplement or a calcium meal for ½ - 1 hour
For 1% of women Excessively high natural fluoride over 4.0 ppm as designated by the EPA	No fluoride tablets in pregnancy needed unless using bottled water only

FOR INFANTS AND CHILDREN

For infants, especially from birth to two years, it is very easy to give an excessive amount of fluoride, therefore, it is important, when deciding how much tap water your infant or toddler can drink in addition to their daily fluoride supplement, to know how much fluoride there is in the water. If you use bottled water rather than tapfor the baby, then the amount of fluoride in the water doesn't matter.

For people using tap water for the infant, 99 percent of the population live in one of three areas.

1) Fluoride deficient, low-fluoride areas that do not fluoridate the water; 0.4 ppm or less in the water.

2) Fluoridated water from the municipal plant or naturally fluoridated water with 0.5-1.2 ppm.

3) Natural fluoride over 1.2 ppm.

How do you find out in which of these do you live? If you are on a municipal or city water supply, all you have to do is look in the phone book under the listing for the city, look for the water department (water and sewer, etc.), give them a call, and ask what the fluoride content of the water is. If you are on a private water system or a well, usually a phone call to either the closest municipal water system or to the county or state health department will give you the answer. In some cases, it is necessary to have your well water tested, which usually can be done free of charge at the county or state Health Department laboratory.

Note: *ppm* (parts per million) is a scientific term. It is not necessary to understand what it means, but when we have one ppm of fluoride in the water, what it means is that we have one fluoride atom (F) to every million molecules of water (H_2O).

Next, you take the information concerning the amount of fluoride in your water and look up the correct amount on the fluoride table in this chapter in order to determine how much fluoride you should supplement your infant and child to try to perfect their teeth. A more complete discussion is given in Chapters 28 through 37 of this book in the year-by-year guide.

CAUTION

In pregnancy, there is a big leeway in the amount of fluoride that can be given by supplement and the fluoride that can be in the water and diet because the large size of the mother protects the fetus from excess fluoride. In infancy and early childhood, when we give the fluoride directly to the small baby or toddler, we must be exact in the amount given because if we give twice the amount recommended it can cause white stains in the permanent teeth. If we give four times the recommended amount, it can result in brown stains. A dentist can remove most of these stains when the child is 10-16 years old a lot easier than he/she can fill cavities when the child is 2-3 years old when not enough fluoride has been given, but there is no need to give an excess. There has never been a case of tooth staining from taking two fluoride tablets a day during pregnancy. We have never had to remove stains from giving fluoride supplements to infants and children, if the parents followed our directions. *Because caution must be used in the amount of fluoride given to infants, especially the first year of life, and because consideration must be given to such variables as weight, breast feeding, liquid, concentrated, or powdered formula, amount of fluoride in the water, amount of the water drunk, etc., supplement dosage for infants should only be decided upon after reading Chapters 28 and 29.*

INFANTS' AND CHILDREN'S SUPPLEMENTS

Child's Age	Supplement in Drops or Tablets Daily	Fluoride Content of Water
Birth to 6 months (If you took the prenatal fluoride tablets, you can start 2-6 weeks after birth. If not, you must start right away).	Optidose®, by weight dropper for most conservative birth to 15 pound program (see Chapter 28) **or** 1/8 mg (0.125 mg) which is one drop of fluoride drops or ½ dropper of 0.25 mg vitamin-fluoride drops	From birth to 2 years and especially from birth to 1 year, it is important to restrict tap water for the baby if it is fluoridated or has over 0.4 ppm natural fluoride 1) 0.4 ppm or less-no limit 2) 0.5-1.2 ppm areas, limit tap water to less than ½ ounce (15 ml) per pound of baby's weight per day and use mostly bottled water. 3) Over 1.2 ppm, use only bottled water, no tap water at all
6 months to 2 years	1/4 mg (0.25 mg)	Same as above

2 to 3 years	½ mg (0.5 mg)	Can gradually increase tap water use over 2-3 years of age
3 to 6 years	one mg (1.0 mg)	No restrictions after 6 years
7 years through teens	one mg adequate; 2 mg best for molars	No restrictions

Q. Again, how do I find out the fluoride content of our water?

A. Call your municipal water plant. If you use a private well, call you city, county or state Public Health Department. They will know or can test your water for you. If you live in a backward state that is not equipped to do this, have your physician or dentist call Omni Fluoricheck™ at (800) 445-3386. They are good at testing water, but ignore their suggestions for fluoride supplements, as they must follow the Dental Association schedule designed to keep dentists busy.

Q. We live in a fluoridated area but drink bottled water, not tap water. What schedule should I follow for my children?

A. Use the schedule for a non-fluoridated area with less than 0.5 ppm.

Q. I nurse my children. What schedule should I use?

A. Almost no fluoride is in the mother's milk, whether she is drinking fluoridated water or not. Even if she takes fluoride tablets while nursing, almost none gets through to the milk. Therefore, the nursing mother should put the fluoride directly into the baby, using the dosage schedule for an unfluoridated area, 1/8 mg to 6 months and then ¼ mg to 2 years. Restrict the use of fluoridated tap water, either drunk directly in a bottle or mixed with formula supplement, to ½ ounce (15 ml) per pound of the baby's weight per day. Use bottled water for the rest or use all bottled water. (See Chapters 28 and 29).

Q. My dentist or physician showed me the label on the fluoride or fluoride-vitamin bottle, and it says to give less than this dosage schedule. Why is that?

A. The dosage on the labeling on the bottle is an attempt to equal the amount of fluoride that we think the average child gets from fluoridated water, which will reduce cavities by 50-60 percent. That dosage has to be low because although we can control the concentration of fluoride in the water, we cannot control how much water any person drinks. There are always a few children in the community who drink large amounts of tap water. Therefore, we have to keep the concentration of fluoride in fluoridated water low enough so that they will not receive an excess amount no matter how much water they drink. By supplementing with drops or tablets, we have control over exactly how much is being given; therefore, we can get closer to the ideal dosage and, by doing so, we can try to perfect the children's teeth. So, what you tell your dentist or physician is that the labeling on the bottle is very nice but that's for only a 50-60 percent improvement in the children's teeth. You wish to have 100 percent improvement in the children's teeth; therefore, you wish to supplement according to this schedule. We will tell you how to do this with or without your dentist's or physician's cooperation later.

Q My physician or dentist showed me the new labeling on the fluoride-vitamin drops that says the fluoride supplement should start at 6 months, why is that?

A. From 1950 to 1994, the standard of care in this country required that fluoride supplements start at or shortly after birth. This was because all studies showed that the permanent teeth were more resistant to cavities the earlier the fluoride was started. In 1982, the American Dental Association (ADA) gave up the pretense of caring about the public and declared that its first priority was to increase the busyness of its dentist members. They began a campaign to reduce fluoride for children. They now insist that fluoride supplements not be given until 6 months of age when the front baby teeth are already fully formed. They wanted these teeth to contain no fluoride which will result in the teeth being as soft as possible. These soft teeth can easily decay just from breast milk, and as the parents cannot help but see the enlarging brown and black cavities in the front teeth, they will bring the child to the dentist and begin a lifetime of drill and fill dependency with your friendly ADA dentist (see Chapter 25).

Q. If I follow this schedule, is it necessary to do anything else in order for the children not to have cavities?

A. The fluoride schedule in this book will produce teeth with such strong enamel that they will withstand almost any abuse. However, depending on heredity, diet and mouth care, even a strong fluoride tooth could eventually show some possible damage. Therefore, some attention to diet control and home care; that is, brushing etc., is, of course, to be advised, in addition to taking the proper amount of fluoride. This will be covered in Chapter 6, Additional Prevention Methods.

CHAPTER THREE

SHORT REVIEW OF THE EVIDENCE FOR THE BENEFITS OF PRENATAL FLUORIDE

A more detailed review of the evidence for prenatal fluoride is in the appendix.

Prenatal water fluoridation studies: There are six large studies involving tens of thousands of children that compared children whose mothers used fluoridated water from the start of their pregnancies with children whose first use of fluoridated water was from birth. Three of these were the classic trials of the 1940s, whose results were used to justify adopting water fluoridation as official US Public Health policy. These studies found an additional 10 to 35% reduction in cavities in the children whose exposure to fluoride began in pregnancy.

Prenatal fluoride tablet supplementation (PNF) studies: There are ten fluoride pregnancy tablet studies in the literature, with seven involving large numbers of children, while three are small reports. The seven large trials found from 30 to 99% reduction in cavities from PNF and the three small reports found 100% of the PNF children had no cavities.

Confirming objective evidence from the examination of PNF and non-PNF teeth: Determinations of the fluoride content of the enamel of PNF teeth, in the US and in Germany, have found that only the PNF teeth contain the amount of fluoride that the US Dental Public Health Service in 1950 recognized as the amount necessary to have teeth that would not decay. Non-PNF teeth contain less than 1/3 that amount. Independent observations in Sweden and in the US found that fluoride sufficient molars have smoother, naturally sealed chewing surfaces which are much less likely to decay.

Fluoride's pre-eruptive effect on tooth quality: It has been known for almost 50 years that the fluoride that is given in the first year or two of life has a large positive effect on the permanent teeth that begin to develop after birth, but that do not appear in the mouth until 5 to 9 years later. This is the pre-eruptive or lag effect of fluoride and it has to do with the fact that it is the amount of fluoride present at the earliest stage of tooth development that largely determines the amount of fluoride that is built into the enamel during the final stage of mineralization just before the tooth erupts. Even if an adequate amount of fluoride is supplied during that final stage of development, the tooth can use very little of it unless an adequate amount of fluoride was present during early development. Drs. Light, Bibby, and Glenn in the US, Dr. Kunzel in Germany with Australia's Dr. Schamshula, have all demonstrated that this same pre-eruptive lag effect holds true for the fetal teeth as well.

"Medical" benefits from PNF—birth statistics, growth, and development: There are many animal studies showing poor growth and poor health resulting from inadequate fluoride. There is some information in humans. The Harvard School of Public Health found improved pregnancy outcomes with increased fluoride in the water. A 1982 study in the *American Journal of Obstetrics & Gynecology* found PNF associated with reduced prematurity and a slight increase in birth weight. NIH found a 16% reduction of prematurity with PNF and slightly increased birth weight. The World Health Organization reported improved growth for PNF infants in 1996. Fluoride is not a growth stimulant any more than is calcium or iron, but the birth weight is a marker for good nutrition, and if any essential nutrient is not sufficiently supplied, the fetus—infant—child will not grow or develop to her or his full genetic potential.

Others who advise PNF: In Australia, PNF has been used as a public health measure for many years. Professors Kailis and Pritchard, and Dr. Noel Martin, Dean of the University of Sydney Dental School have been strong supporters. In Scotland, Professor of Oral Medicine at the University of Glasgow's Dental School, K.W. Stephen, has had the Obstetric Unit at their Medical School use PNF since 1975. Dr. Itzak Gedalia, Professor of Oral Biology at the Hadassah-Hebrew Dental School in Jerusalem, the "grand old man" of European fluoride research, started recommending PNF in his lectures in 1987. Professor Gedalia has a most distinguished career in research, teaching, and writing, and has received all honors possible in his profession, including being elected President of the International Association for Dental Research. It is his judgment that the evidence for the need for PNF has existed since the 1960s. It is our hope and prayer that Professor Gedalia is too distinguished and universally honored for NIDCR (formally NIDR), at NIH, to dare attempt to harm him professionally for his outspoken honesty.

CHAPTER FOUR

PRENATAL FLUORIDE AND YOUR PREGNANCY—NURSE, FAMILY DOCTOR/OBSTETRICIAN

In order for your child to have the strongest possible teeth, you must start taking fluoride tablets by the twelfth week of your pregnancy. You may want to let your physician know about taking fluoride as a mineral supplement. Before we tell you the three basic reactions that physicians may have to the subject of prenatal fluoride, we should remind you of the following facts.

1. Medical doctors, including obstetricians, only know about fluoride what they've been told by the American Dental Association. Fluoride is considered a "dental mineral." Physicians in medical school do not study fluoride as they do iron, calcium and vitamins.

2. Obstetricians are highly nervous these days, as in the past twenty years they have gone from "the most beloved doctors" to "the most sued doctors." What society has allowed lawyers and judges to do to them is a tragedy and we are all paying for it, as your doctor must pass his/her $10,000.00 a month insurance and legal expense on to you, the patient.

3. Many obstetricians do not yet consider that the quality of the child's teeth is their responsibility. The soft, fluoride deficient teeth hidden in the baby's gums at birth actually is a birth defect due to a nutritional deficiency during pregnancy. However, since almost all children have such teeth, it is thought to be normal and since the teeth are not seen until the child is 6 months to 2 years old, the soft teeth are not yet considered to be the birth defect that they are. Your doctor's

attitude towards prenatal fluoride will be represented by one of the following quotations:

a. "Good idea. I encourage my patients to supplement all of the essential vitamins and minerals when pregnant."

b. "I don't really know that much about it. It's up to you."

c. "I don't recommend it."

Let us examine each of these answers and learn what it may tell you about your doctor.

A. *"Good idea. I encourage my patients to supplement all of the essential vitamins and minerals when pregnant."* This doctor knows that your nutrition during pregnancy is the most important factor determining the health of your baby. He/She knows that there are three essential nutrients that the "normal, well balanced diet" will not give you enough of during pregnancy - the three F's; folate (folic acid), ferrous (iron) and fluoride. She also knows that it is difficult to get enough calcium and riboflavin so she sees to it that you supplement these nutrients in order to have a better baby. He is aware how folic acid was neglected in the 1970s and 1980s, which resulted in 2,000 babies born per year with unnecessary brain and spinal birth defects. This doctor may also have known some of the following facts.

1. There have been ten studies done all over the world showing that prenatal fluoride supplement tablets can greatly benefit children's teeth. Four test studies were done in the United States starting in the 1950s.

2. Hundreds of thousands of Australian pregnant women have been given fluoride as a routine public health measure starting in the late 1940s.

3. The Food and Drug Administration, the American Medical Association, and the American Dental Association have never questioned the safety of fluoride in pregnancy.

4. A report in the American Journal of Obstetrics and Gynecology in 1982 found that prenatal fluoride babies were slightly larger and had less prematurity than those babies not supplemented with fluoride. The same reduction of prematurity was found by our National Institutes of Health (NIH) in their prenatal fluoride supplement program in Maine.

This doctor is highly knowledgeable and very likely to be a superior obstetrician.

B. *"I don't really know that much about it. It's up to you."* This is the only honest answer the majority of physicians can give, but few doctors like to admit that they don't know something. A doctor who is sufficiently secure to say this is likely to be a good physician and probably deserves your trust.

C. *"I don't recommend it."* This doctor may actually be an antifluoridationist. He or she is not knowledgeable about nutrition and may not keep up with medical developments. Instead of saying "I don't know," he or she says, "No." The doctor, whether age 30 or 60, is a relic from earlier times when it was customary for physicians to pretend to know it all. We would worry about the quality of this doctor's advice in other areas as well.

Try to see it from your doctor's point of view. He or she is supposed to be an expert about pregnancy, but they know little or nothing about fluoride and even less about teeth development. They are annoyed someone is asking about a subject of which they are mostly ignorant. They are even more annoyed that someone is trying to make them responsible for the kid's teeth for goodness sake! That is for dentists! Human nature makes them say, "No."

The third to fourth months of pregnancy are your last opportunity to give your future child really great baby teeth and the fifth-sixth months are the last chance to give your future child a rare lifetime gift of super white, smooth six year molars. When your child is an elderly woman or man, when you are no longer here, she or he will nostalgically bless you for loving her or him enough, even before birth, to provide all the nutrients needed. The only recognized nutrient that cannot be adequately obtained in the food and drink of even the best possible diet is fluoride.(The others discussed earlier can be, with difficulty) The authors each now have over 40 years experience providing fluoride supplements in pregnancy and have received nothing but thanks from the thousands of persons involved—for over two generations. When you finish reading this book, you will know more about this subject than will your physician or your dentist, so you are the most qualified to decide to give your child the best possible teeth.

In any case, at the present time, the responsibility for the quality of your child's teeth rests with you, not your physician. At the present time, they can claim that it is officially not their job, although it is going to be increasingly difficult for them to ignore this responsibility since the Food and Nutrition Board has recognized that 3 mg of fluoride a day is the minimum amount for adaquate intake in pregnancy. As the amount of fluoride in the diet, including fluoridated water, in the US ranges from 0.5 to 2.0 mg/day, a fluoride supplement is required to avoid a nutritional deficiency with a resultant birth defect, and that is why, just as with folic acid, it will soon be your physician's official responsibility to see that you take fluoride supplements in pregnancy. The Food & Drug Administration has just been forced to admit, via our Congressman, David Weldon, MD, that prenatal fluoride may be sold under the Dietary Supplement Health Education Act (DSHEA). We should not underestimate, however, the power of the Dental Association's and Dental Industry's Washington lobby. With few exceptions, dentists are horrified at the prospect that physicians can eliminate the disease that they primarily live on.

CHAPTER FIVE

HOW TO GET THE FLUORIDE YOU NEED IN YOUR PREGNANCY AND PREGNANCY NUTRITION

Fluoride, for the past 50 years, has been the only essential nutrient for which you need a prescription in the USA. You can buy all other minerals and vitamins in the drug store, health food store and the grocery store. This requirement has nothing to do with safety as we are warned not to take excessive vitamins A and D, or excessive calcium and iron, and none of these require a prescription. A prescription has been required because, unlike the other minerals, fluoride was introduced to the public, as water fluoridation, by the Government and the Government never gave up control. The safety of fluoride is not a problem as they put it in the public water supply and allow a highly concentrated amount in toothpaste, fluoride rinses, etc.

You can buy calcium fluoride without a prescription but it is not nearly as good as it does not provide you with much calcium or fluoride as these two minerals stay strongly bound together and goes right through your intestinal tract like a rock. The proper procedure is to take the calcium and the sodium fluoride at different times of day and let them combine in the teeth and bones to make them as strong as marble rock.

In 1994, Congress passed a deregulation type law that actually freed the US a little from this Big Brother control of our children's nutrition and well-being. Called the Dietary Supplement Health and Education Act (DSHEA), it allows anything that has to do with diet and nutrition to be sold without a prescription as a supplement as long as no health claims are made for it. Thus, a 2 or 3 mg fluoride tablet can be sold now just like iron and calcium and all other nutrients. At the time of publication, however, these supplement tablets have not yet been made and until they come on the market, you must get the 1 mg tablets (2.2 mg of sodium fluoride) made for children and take 2 at one time.

Where to get your fluoride prescription:

1. *Your dentist:* Your children's dentist or family dentist, if he or she is a quality dentist, will give you a fluoride prescription for your pregnancy. As far back as 1982, in a survey done by the American Dental Association, American dentists believed, by a ratio of 2 to 1, that fluoride supplements should start at pregnancy, so you should have no problem finding a dentist who is interested in real prevention. If your own dentist only wants to sell you fluoride treatments, plastic sealants, and fillings, but will not help you build fluoride into your children's teeth, get another dentist. There is no need to allow yourself and your children to be exploited in that manner.

2. *Your physician:* Your family doctor or obstetrician should help you supplement all essential vitamins and minerals, including fluoride for your pregnancy.

3. *Your pharmacist:* In most of Europe, in Florida, and hopefully in some other states, pharmacists are allowed to sell fluoride without a prescription. If your pharmacist is not knowledgeable about prenatal fluoride, get the fluoride for your older children and then take it yourself. If the pharmacist is reluctant to sell you fluoride in a fluoridated community, remind him or her that you may be one of the many families who drink bottled water that is not fluoridated.

4. *Drink rinse:* Fluoride rinses, the type that is sold in supermarkets and drug stores without a prescription, contain 0.05% sodium fluoride. Two teaspoons of rinse supply just over two milligrams of fluoride, the correct daily supplement for pregnancy. Although we would prefer you to get the fluoride tablets, if you cannot get them, take 2 teaspoons (10 ml total) of an <u>alcohol</u> <u>free</u> fluoride

rinse such as ACT™ a day on an empty stomach in the same way we told you to take the tablets.

GENERAL NUTRITION: PREGNANT OR NOT

Perhaps our discussion of preventive nutrition has inspired you to become more knowledgeable and more involved in your overall nutrition, especially while pregnant. If so, good! Where should you go for sensible advice? That's easy, consult the one nutritionist in this country who has been consistently right in her judgment during the past 20 years while all of our other nutritionists, including most of those at our most prestigious universities, have been preaching the same false party line, "eat a good balanced diet and there is no need for supplements." They so wanted this claim to be true that they let it affect their judgment and they ignored all evidence to the contrary. Why did they all do this? Because the statement is almost true and because they were understandably repulsed by the false religion of mega-dosing and by the commercial exploitation of the health concerns of the public by some of the "health food" industry. Nutritionist Elizabeth Somer has also preached the proverbial good balanced diet as she recognized those substances such as vitamin C and beta-carotene were markers for foods that contain hundreds to thousands of beneficial compounds that you would not get by eating a fast food/prepared packaged food diet and taking supplements. However, she has always recognized the benefits of sensible supplementation in addition to the "good balanced diet." She was right and most all of her colleagues were wrong.

What proved them wrong? In pregnancy, folic acid (folate) did. Up to 1970, the recommended amount of daily folate, a B vitamin, was 400 mcg (microgram) for prevention of an uncommon megalobastic anemia, especially in pregnancy. The problem was that 400 mcg was almost impossible to get in a good balanced diet and the academic nutritionists did not want to provide any reason for supplementation; so by 1980, ignoring the evidence that had been coming out of England since the late 1960s that folate prevented neural tube birth defects (incomplete spinal cords with paralysis,

31

missing brains with death, etc.), they cut the recommended amount in half to 200 mcg. In the mid 1980s, a woman nutritionist from one of the most prestigious universities in California wrote the nutrition chapter in one of our most revered obstetrics textbooks. She discussed folate only in terms of anemia and decided no supplement was necessary, never mentioning the, by then, numerous papers published about neural tube defect prevention. Ten years later, the nutritional establishment was forced to admit that they had been responsible for 2,000 serious birth defects a year in this country alone and they raised folate back to 400 mcg and made plans to put it in bread. Some of those who had for 30 years denied the need for extra folate now write how terrible it is that "ignorant" women get pregnant without taking folate supplements.

What proved the anti-supplement academics wrong in general nutrition? Good old vitamin C (ascorbic acid), the first mega-dose vitamin thanks to Dr. Linus Pauling, the recipient of two Nobel Prizes, among others. For most of the past half century, the official line on vitamin C was that an adult needed 60 mg a day.(In some countries it was as low as 12 mg!) Most of us in the medical profession assumed that the ascorbic people were competent and knew what they were talking about. It didn't seem that difficult a subject. Suddenly, 16 years ago, they say, "sorry, 60 mg is the amount needed to keep you from having actual active scurvy (gums bleeding, hair falling out, terminal fatigue, etc.), 240 mg is the amount needed to saturate the tissues." Well, thank you so much, only off by 400% for 40 years. There is a nice mathematical symmetry there, but you have made good people seem foolish. Later in the book, we will revisit the subject as to why it seems increasingly that our lives are in the hands of undeserving persons.

Nutritionist Elizabeth Somer is consultant to ABCs "Good Morning America," Advisory Board Member of "Shape Magazine," and Editor of "Nutrition Alert," an excellent bi-monthly newsletter by Nutrition Communications, 4742 Liberty Road S, Suite 148, Salem, OR 97302 for only $15 a year or go to www.elizabethsomer.com. She also has written five books, *Food and Mood, The Essential*

Guide to Vitamins and Minerals, Age Proof Your Body, Nutrition for Women, and *Nutrition for a Healthy Pregnancy.* That is the one you need for your pregnancy. It was published by Holt in 1995 and Amazon.com gave it its highest rating, deservedly so.

Picture of Child with Prenatal Fluoride Supplement Teeth

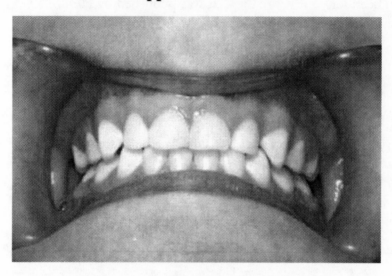

Picture of Child with No Prenatal Fluoride Supplement American Dental Association Teeth

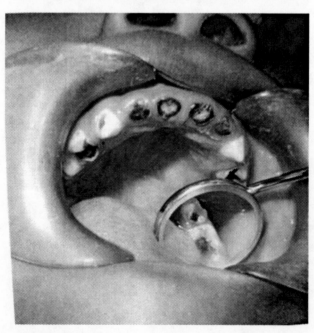

Surface Enamel of Primary Teeth with
Prenatal Fluoride Supplement
(electron microscope)

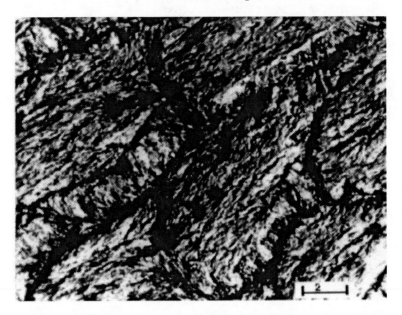

The 'paving stone' forms you see are the surface ends of the enamel prisms or rods that make up the hard mineral part of the teeth. The density of the enamel crystals making up the prisms is indicated by the degree of darkness present. Even more important, is the narrow darkness between the large prisms. This tells us that there is little or no space for soft organic (mostly proteins) tooth structure between the prisms. There are no "toe holds" for mouth germs and their acid to gain access to these teeth.

Surface Enamel of Primary Teeth with No Prenatal Fluoride Supplement (electron microscope)

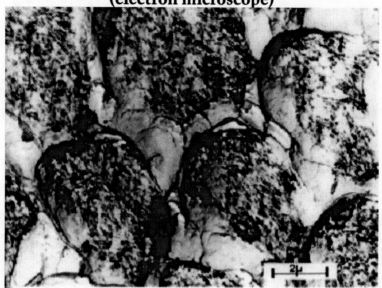

Here, the surface ends of the enamel prism are lighter, indicating a lack of density due to poor mineral formation. Most important, are the large soft spaces between the prisms filled with whitish organic (proteins) tooth material which gives mouth germs an ideal spot to attach themselves and then proceed to melt holes in the tooth with the acid they produce. These teeth, produced by following Dental Association advice, are so soft that even an ideal breast milk nursing diet can cause massive decay.

SUMMARY OF CAVITY IMMUNE TEETH

1. Teeth that contain an ideal amount of fluoride are about 10 times as resistant to cavities as compared to regular fluoride deficient teeth.

2. It is the amount of fluoride that is supplied during the early stage of tooth development that mainly determines how much fluoride will be built into the enamel during the later stage of tooth development, not the amount of fluoride that is being given during the later stage.

3. This early (secretory) stage of development occurs during pregnancy for all the primary (baby) teeth and for the 6 year (1st permanent) molars.

4. Because a pregnant woman so rapidly absorbs fluoride into her bones and excretes it in her urine, fluoridated water cannot deliver the amount of fluoride needed by the fetal teeth, so it is necessary for the mother-to-be to take a once a day supplement of at least 2 mg of fluoride starting the 3rd month.

This information has been well documented in the dental literature over the past 45 years, so why does the dental industry pretend that they don't know or don't understand it? A statement attributed to Upton Sinclair in the 1920s explains it.

It is difficult to get a man to understand something when his salary depends on his not understanding it.

CHAPTER SIX

ADDITIONAL CAVITY PREVENTION METHODS

Taking the proper amount of fluoride in pregnancy and childhood will produce teeth that are almost impossible to decay, but for additional protection, we should continue to use common sense in caring for the teeth after they erupt into the mouth. These protection methods are covered in more detail in Section V, Chapters 28-37, the yearly guide and checklist for parents.

1. *Avoid abuse of the bottle:* Never put a baby to bed with formula, milk, or sweet drinks in the bottle—only give water in the bottle to drink in bed.

2. *Diet control:* Good nutrition is important for the child's health as well as for the teeth, so some control should be kept over what the child eats and drinks.

3. *Brushing the teeth:* When the child is old enough to rinse and spit and not swallow the toothpaste, usually at 2½-3 years, start brushing with a fluoride toothpaste. Before the child can be trusted to rinse and spit, use only water on the toothbrush or use a non-fluoride toothpaste such as Baby OraGel™. For children under age three who can rinse and spit well enough to use a fluoride toothpaste use a <u>pinhead</u> amount of fluoride toothpaste— not a ribbon the length of the toothbrush. Since our fluoride supplement program gives the infant and child 90-100 percent of the ideal amount of fluoride, we do not want the young child (especially birth to 3 years) to swallow much additional fluoride. From 3 years to 6 years, use a small pea-sized amount. After age 6, they can use more toothpaste if they wish, but it still should be spit out when they are finished brushing.

4. ***Professional care:*** Starting about age 3, the dentist should be cleaning the teeth every 6 months for the health of the teeth and gums and those cleanings can be followed by fluoride gel in a tray treatment.

Photograph of the chewing surface
of a molar produced with
Prenatal Fluoride Supplement

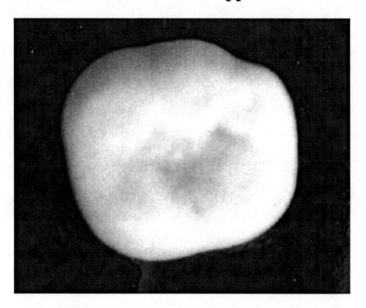

The fluoride taken during pregnancy, when this molar starts to develop from the top down, allows the four cusps (the high areas) to coalesce together and form a naturally sealed surface, without deep crevices in which food and bacteria can hide and cause hidden decay. Ninety five percent of children have the genetic ability to produce molars like this if adequate fluoride is provided from the start of their formation.

Frances B. Glenn, DDS, William D. Glenn III, MD

Photograph of the chewing surface of a molar produced with No Prenatal Fluoride Supplement

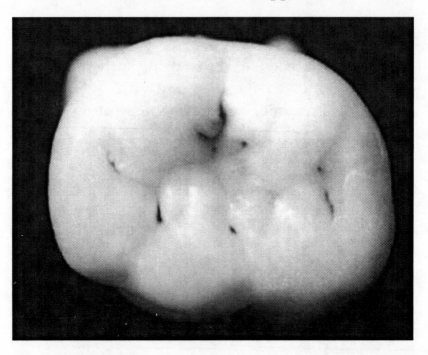

The deep crevices and fissures seen here are typical of those molars produced without prenatal fluoride. The failure of the cusps (high areas) to flow together fully is a birth defect caused by a nutritional deficiency during pregnancy, analogous to the failure of the spinal cord to close properly when folic acid is withheld. These molars require immediate sealant treatment. The sealant is a temporary plastic surface filling which makes the child totally dependent upon dentists as they start down the road to drill, fill, fill and refill, crowns, and root canals.

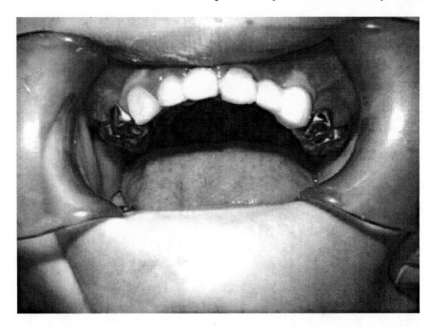

This child's mother did not take fluoride supplements when pregnant and the child's soft fluoride deficient American Dental Association teeth melted away when he ate and drank. They have been expertly repaired: four crowns, three caps, and a 3-unit bridge. Dental fee: $2,000 - $2,500. No wonder the Dental Association advises that children have these defective teeth. Cost for outpatient OR and anesthesia: $2,500 - $3,000. Total cost: over $5,000, to say nothing of the discomfort and risks involved. All could have been prevented for a few dollars worth of mineral supplement while pregnant.

No fluoride toothpaste until a child is old enough to rinse and spit, then just a pea-sized amount under age 6.

Rover is old enough to use lots of paste now, Mom!

CHAPTER SEVEN

OTHER FACTS ABOUT FLUORIDE

I. Fluoride is different from all other essential minerals in that the fluoride that is in food is mostly bound up in protein and calcium complexes and that "bound" fluoride cannot be used by the teeth and bones in the body. Fluoride is the only essential mineral, which we normally obtain in water because in water it dissolves and is, therefore, available to be used in building strong teeth and bones. Besides being available in water, it is available as a supplement in the form of sodium fluoride. The sodium in sodium fluoride is such a small amount that it is negligible. A 2.2-milligram (mg) sodium fluoride tablet gives us 1 mg of fluoride and 1.2 mg of sodium. If a pregnant woman is taking two of these, she is getting 2.4 mg of sodium. A low sodium diet contains 2,000 mg of sodium a day and a normal diet contains 5,000 mg of sodium a day, therefore, the amount of sodium you are getting when you take sodium fluoride is of no importance at all because it is such a small amount. The closest material to sodium fluoride with which you are familiar is sodium chloride, or table salt.

II. The other unusual thing about fluoride, as compared to other essential minerals, is that, as you increase the amount that children take in each day, the quality of the teeth improves, even as you get into a large dose, which can cause some staining of the teeth. With all other minerals, there is an amount, which we can say, is enough and then there is another very much larger amount, which we can say, is too much. This is true of iron, calcium, chloride, potassium, etc. With fluoride, there is no gap between the amount that does the most good and the amount that starts to be excessive. Only in pregnancy is there a leeway or gap between these two amounts.

43

The amount in pregnancy that does the most good is 2-4 mg of supplement with or without the 1 mg that is assumed to be obtained from drinking fluoridated water. We have long experience with two mgs a day but do not know if 3 or 4 mg a day would give more benefit. The amount that would seem to be excessive to us is somewhere between 5 and 10 mg of fluoride a day in pregnancy, and it is reassuring that the official US Food and Nutrition Board says 3 mg is a minimum and 10 mg a maximum a day in pregnancy. Pregnancy is such an excellent time to take fluoride, for two reasons:

1. There is a good leeway in the amount, which you can take.

2. Pregnancy is when all the primary (baby) teeth and six year, (first permanent) molars are forming. These six-year molars traditionally have had the most decay of any of the permanent teeth in the body because they were the least supplied with fluoride. These soft fluoride deficient baby teeth and 6-year molars are responsible for "the cavity prone years of childhood." This phrase was coined by dentists to make you think it is normal for children's teeth to have cavities. In infancy, especially between birth and two years, and somewhat between two and five years of age, there is very little leeway and we have to be very cautious about the amount that the infant gets in the developing permanent teeth. As we have said, there is no possibility of causing tooth staining (fluorosis) by taking fluoride in pregnancy with any reasonable dose of fluoride. The dosage we have suggested is less than one third to one fourth of the amount that is required to produce any kind of even mild white flecks in the primary teeth. It is possible in the Northern part of this country, in areas that are fluoridated at 1 ppm or above, that if the very young child drinks a lot of tap water and takes a full supplement dosage, it might result in some tooth stain, so limit the tap water. (The 1/8th mg/day supplement we start with is only 1/4th the amount that was officially used prior to 1979.) If the child is especially small or is a heavy drinker of fluoridated tap - straight or mixed with formula - water, then

the daily use of tap water should be restricted to less than ½ ounce per pound of body weight. If the child gets excessive fluoride from birth to 5 years, and develops some stains in the permanent teeth, these can be removed by a dentist, if need be, when the child is 10-16 years old. Taking fluoride tablets in pregnancy allows us to permit a significantly smaller fluoride dose in infancy which should further reduce the possibility of staining in the front permanent teeth as these "smile teeth" develop at that time.

Q.   Does taking fluoride tablets in pregnancy interfere with any other method of dental prevention?

A.   No, pregnancy fluoride tablets do not conflict with water fluoridation, fluoride toothpaste, or dental fluoride treatments.

CHAPTER EIGHT

PRIMARY TEETH, PERMANENT TEETH, GINGIVA:

What Do We Mean, And What Causes And Prevents Tooth Decay?

The twenty primary teeth, meaning first set of teeth have also been called baby teeth, milk teeth, and deciduous teeth. They start to develop about the 12th week of pregnancy, appear in the mouth starting about age 6 months and are usually all in between 2½ and 3½ years.

Primary Teeth Chart

Upper (Maxillary) Teeth	Appears (Erupts)	Lost (Shed)
Center incisor	7-12 months	6-7 years
Lateral incisor	8-13	7-8
Cuspid (eye, canine)	16-22	10-12
1st (primary) molar	12-19	9-11
2nd (primary) molar	24-32	10-12
Lower (mandibular) teeth	Have the same names as the uppers and have about the same erupt/shed schedule as do the uppers except the central incisors are usually the first teeth to erupt at 5-10 months.	

Twenty-eight of the 32 permanent teeth begin development at or after birth. The four first permanent (6 year) molars are really the third molars of the primary teeth and they begin to develop at the start of the 5th month of pregnancy. If fluoride is not provided until birth, these four teeth, the most important in the mouth, will almost always need fillings.

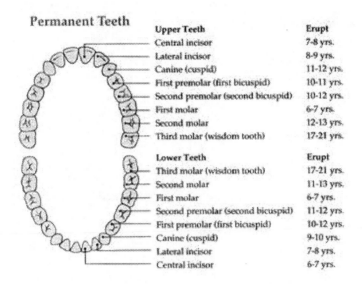

Permanent Teeth

Upper Teeth	Erupt
Central incisor	7-8 yrs.
Lateral incisor	8-9 yrs.
Canine (cuspid)	11-12 yrs.
First premolar (first bicuspid)	10-11 yrs.
Second premolar (second bicuspid)	10-12 yrs.
First molar	6-7 yrs.
Second molar	12-13 yrs.
Third molar (wisdom tooth)	17-21 yrs.

Lower Teeth	Erupt
Third molar (wisdom tooth)	17-21 yrs.
Second molar	11-13 yrs.
First molar	6-7 yrs.
Second premolar (second bicuspid)	11-12 yrs.
First premolar (first bicuspid)	10-12 yrs.
Canine (cuspid)	9-10 yrs.
Lateral incisor	7-8 yrs.
Central incisor	6-7 yrs.

Gingiva is the medical/dental name for the gums—the soft pink tissue that covers the ridge of jawbone that holds the teeth in your mouth. The gingiva is attached to the teeth just below the free edge of the gingiva, which also surrounds the teeth but is not attached. It is in this space between the free edge or flap of the gingiva and the tooth that stuff accumulates and causes gingivitis which is Latin for inflammation of the gingiva. Gingiva is actually the exact Latin word for the gums. If you were in Rome anytime between 700 BC and the present, walk up to a local and say, "gingiva," you would be understood. Do we have to apologize for using the word gum or gums? Not at all, as it is a real Old English word derived from the North German (which is where the original English language came from before William the Conqueror brought his French/Latin with him when he took over in 1066. William and his Norman knights were descended from Vikings who had been in the Normandy peninsula of France for some 200 years) word, *gome, goma,* which comes from the Old Norse (Viking), *gomr.*

Now if we say gum as in chewing gum or in describing soft gummy stuff from a tree or plant, are we using the same word? No, as that gum comes from the Old French, gomme, which came from the Latin, gommi, which came from the Greek, kommi, which they got from the Egyptian, qmy.

Q. What does this have to do with teeth?

A. Very little.

Q. Then why is it in the chapter?

A. Two reasons: 1) We got about as bored writing the teeth charts as you did reading them and needed a small diversion. 2) Most of our readers are younger and we thought they would like to be reminded how One World, New Age, Cosmically Related everything is. Whatever.

FACTORS THAT ALLOW AND PREVENT TOOTH DECAY

I.   HEREDITY

Before the fluoride era officially began in 1945, approximately 2% (2 out of every 100 persons) of the people, who did not live in natural high fluoride areas, were immune to dental cavities as the result of inborn genetic factors that mostly ran in families. You would think that dental researchers would have studied these fortunate few in order to find what kept their teeth from decaying so that they might help the 98% who had cavities, but they did not. During the first half of the twentieth century, the subject that interested dentists most was the concept of "extend to prevent." To their delight, they showed that instead of just filling a small cavity, the tooth would last longer if the dentist drilled out and filled the surrounding grooves, fissures and other cavity prone areas near the small cavity. This dental "Vietnam War" strategy—save the tooth by largely destroying it, or "proceed to a crown as rapidly as possible," actually did improve dental health, and was even of greater benefit for dentists' incomes.

Back to heredity, in the early 1970s in Yugoslavia, a dental researcher did x-ray diffraction studies of tooth enamel from persons immune to decay and found a very tight crystalline structure as compared to enamel from persons not immune to decay. A similar tight density of the enamel was reported by R. LeGeros, D. Lee, and F. Glenn in *The Journal of Dental Research* in 1985 in the primary tooth enamel of children whose mothers had taken fluoride supplements while pregnant. As the lead researcher and author, New York University's Racquel LeGeros, has a peerless international reputation in this rarified field of mineralized tissue (teeth and bones) research, the dental establishment dealt with this report, not with their usual attack, but by ignoring it.

Hereditary factors

2. *Enamel quality*—density, tightness
3. *Saliva quality*—some spit is better than others
4. *Immune factors*—dealing with mouth germs that make acid from food

II. ENVIRONMENT DURING TOOTH DEVELOPMENT

Mother's diet is first and foremost. She needs all recognized nutrients that are necessary for producing the best possible baby: protein (amino acids), carbohydrates, a few essential fatty acids, and vitamins, especially folic acid even before getting pregnant, iron, calcium (if not enough calcium, the fetus usually gets it from the mother's bones, not her teeth), and the usual trace minerals, magnesium, zinc, selenium etc. Everything mentioned so far can be obtained in the proverbial good balanced diet and with a standard daily prenatal (pregnancy) supplement capsule. There is one other essential nutrient that is absolutely necessary for producing the best possible teeth, and not anything close to the minimum amount of this nutrient recommended by the Food and Nutrition Board of the American Academy of Sciences in Washington, DC during pregnancy can be obtained unless it is taken as a supplement. By now, you certainly know the name of the missing essential nutrient! Fluoride. Two milligrams taken once a day taken on an empty stomach at a separate time from the prenatal vitamin-mineral capsule and not followed by food, especially calcium food such as milk or cheese for at least 30-60 minutes. Got that memorized? Good!

Environment during development

1. Fluoride supplement, prenatal & postnatal
2. Good diet

3. Prenatal vitamin-mineral capsule
4. No alcohol, tobacco, or illegal drugs
5. Minimal medicines, especially first three months of pregnancy
6. Illness, especially in childhood can affect tooth enamel—"high fever" white spots

Before we finish up by listing factors affecting tooth decay after the teeth are in the mouth, permit us a few words concerning items 1-4 in the above pregnancy list. Some of you may be thinking "jeez, these people are some Puritans; not even alcohol." Although we have never used alcohol as a daily after work relaxant, we do, usually on the weekend, use some alcohol socially. Alcohol is toxic and if we choose as non-pregnant adults to knock out some brain cells, you would agree that is our business. Your doctor may tell you that an occasional glass of wine in pregnancy is okay and it may possibly be, but as we know that women who drink regularly while pregnant often produce a brain damaged, deformed child, why take the chance? If you are not willing to give up a few chemical pleasures for nine months, how are you going to make a 20-year commitment to be a responsible parent? We hope the fact that you are reading this book means that you will make and fulfill that commitment, but we all know that too many of the general public will not. Let us suggest to you that creating new life is the most important thing that people do in their lives.

Most of our great literature, from The Books of *Genesis* and *Job*, through Dante, Milton, and Shakespeare, to *War and Peace*, and *Moby-Dick*, is a lament, sometimes a large whine, about having been created and then seemingly abandoned by The Creator, and/or is about our attempt to reconnect with that Creator/Creating Force. There is little we can do about how the universe was set up 13.4 billion or 6,011 years ago, depending upon your point of view, but you can avoid being an abandoning creator yourself. If you are not sincere in making a 9 month/20 year commitment, then you should do yourselves, and especially your potential kid a really big cosmic favor, and not get pregnant in the first place.

III.   ENVIRONMENT AFTER THE TEETH ARE IN THE MOUTH

Continue fluoride supplements until all the teeth are fully erupted. After water fluoridation, postnatal fluoride supplements combined with children's vitamins (developed and promoted by three pediatricians), and fluoride toothpaste, the next most important cause of the reduction in cavities in children's teeth since WW II has been the use of antibiotics by family doctors and pediatricians to avoid the ear and lung complications of childhood colds and other respiratory infections. This antibiotic use, now under some partially excess criticism, has reduced the population of acid forming germs in kid's mouths. Also, mothers are more knowledgeable and there has been a reduction in the use of hard sugar candies that stay in the mouth so long.

Environment after tooth development

1. Childhood fluoride supplements
2. Antibiotics—good side effect from "overuse"
3. Diet control—limit sugar food and drinks
4. Home tooth care—cleaning teeth with fluoride free toothpaste until can rinse, spit really well; then twice a day fluoride toothpaste, but no more than pea size until age 6 years.
5. Professional care—cleanings/fluoride gel at the dental office.

CHAPTER NINE

CHOOSING A QUALITY DENTIST FOR YOUR CHILDREN

What type of dentist can serve your children best?

Ideally, for convenience and in order to have one person responsible, along with yourself, for the care of your children's teeth, the best situation is a pediatric dentist who is fully qualified to do the orthodontics that the child may require as well. However, there are less than five thousand pediatric dentists in this country and, of these, less than 20 percent are qualified to do full orthodontics, therefore, this is not a practical solution for the majority of the children of this country.

A second consideration would be a family dentist who is qualified to do orthodontics and here you also might be able to obtain all of your children's dental treatment with one dentist. For most persons, a family dentist or pediatric dentist who works either in the same office or on a referral basis with an orthodontist will be the arrangement that they will have to use. This is perfectly satisfactory and can result in good dental care as long as the dentists involved are practicing *quality dentistry*. This is the primary consideration no matter what type of dentist your children use. We will tell you what constitutes *quality dentistry*, so that you will be able to choose the proper dentist for your children.

Quality Dentistry for Children

Quality dentistry for children is not difficult and can be done in small rural towns as well as big cities. We will list the requirements and you will see for yourself that it is not too much to expect of the dentist who is helping you care for your children's mouths.

Requirements for Quality Dentistry

1. ***The dentist encourages fluoride supplements for you during pregnancy and prescribes for all your children, both those under his care and for the younger children that are not yet old enough to visit the office.*** As you know, the major part of the quality of the tooth enamel for all the permanent teeth, other than the wisdom teeth, is determined before your child is three years old. In 1982, a survey by the American Dental Association found that American dentists, by a ratio of almost 2 to 1, thought that fluoride supplement should begin in pregnancy rather than wait until birth. Therefore, it should not be too difficult to find a dentist who is interested in true prevention and sees to it that you build the proper amount of fluoride into the children's teeth rather than waiting until those teeth start to decay and then selling you fluoride treatments and plastic coatings for these defective teeth. You would not go to a bone doctor who advised against calcium and then sells you leg braces for your children. Nor would you use an eye doctor who withheld vitamin A in pregnancy and then sells you glasses for your child. Of course not! Likewise, there is no need to pay a dentist to mistreat your children and you.

2. ***Preventive and interceptive orthodontics.*** The quality dentist will monitor the development of your children's teeth and will take the time and trouble in order to do small procedures as these teeth come in, in order to make sure that they are as straight as possible. The quality dentist does not let the teeth become a jumbled mess and then refer you to an orthodontist when the child is twelve years old in order to spend a lot of money and time to straighten them out. The quality dentist will see that your child has a panoramic x-ray—this is the type of x-ray where one film goes around the mouth and shows all the teeth. This should be done between age 3 to 5 years as it is the only way to see whether there are missing or extra teeth that are going to affect the way the permanent teeth are going to come into the mouth. If the dentist does not have one of these x-ray machines, he can arrange for you to have this done at an oral surgeon's office. The quality dentist will also file or shave off the side edges of the adjacent baby tooth

in the front of the mouth as the permanent teeth come in if there is not sufficient room. We will go into detail about this procedure in Chapter 13.

3. ***Interceptive or early orthodontics.*** The quality dentist will, either himself/herself or by referral to a dentist who does orthodontics, not let a child whose teeth are grossly protrusive, (buck teeth), wait until the child is twelve years old in order to have them straightened. He will see that these are straightened with a short period of treatment, usually six to nine months, when the child is seven or eight years old. This is so that the teeth will be less likely to be knocked out and so that the child will not develop a poor self-image.

4. If the dentist is a general dentist or pediatric dentist who is also qualified in orthodontics, the dentist should be a member of the American Orthodontic Society, preferably Board-eligible, or a Diplomate of the Board, or have similar qualifications with the International Orthodontic Association.

5. If the dentist is an orthodontist and does nothing but straighten teeth, the dentist should be a member of the American Association of Orthodontics and be eligible for the Board of the American Association of Orthodontics or, preferably, be a Diplomate of the Board.

6. The quality dentist, if your children have not been given sufficient fluoride during pregnancy and early childhood and therefore have teeth that do decay, will make some use of plastic sealants for the molar teeth and, if he must fill a fluoride deficient tooth, the filling should generally stay in and not fall out.

That does not seem too harsh a list of requirements, does it? All we are asking is that the dentist has shown interest in building quality teeth that will have no cavities and won't need fillings, by prescribing fluoride during pregnancy and early childhood, and that the dentist pay some attention to the way the teeth come into the mouth and do a few simple preventive measures so that the teeth will not end up all jumbled up; and that if full orthodontics is required, that the dentist be qualified and use a technique that gets a satisfactory result in an average treatment time of about two years. The requirements for good orthodontics will be discussed in detail in the chapters on Orthodontics.

This, therefore, is a minimum outline for quality dentistry and there is no need for you to accept anything less in this day and time, no matter where you live or what your situation is.

Summing Up

Quality dentistry for children

1. Prescribes fluoride supplements for pregnancy and from birth through the teens so the teeth will have the best possible resistance to cavities.
2. Practices preventive orthodontics and does not allow the teeth to get all jumbled up.

That is not too much to ask, is it?

Not a quality dentist for children

Dr. Silvertongue Wayward-Mossback, T.S.,* F.T.S.,** P.S.S.*** tells mothers-to-be not to take fluoride and does not prescribe it for children, "just bring the kids in four times a year for fluoride treatments and twice a year for plastic sealants and they won't have more than two cavities a year."

* Toothpaste Salesman
** Fluoride Treatment Salesman
*** Plastic Sealant Salesman

How about Quality Dentistry for Adults? Easy enough.

<u>Quality Dentist for Adults</u>

1. Passionate interest in the health of your gums

2. Checks your bite (occlusion) with wax and carbon paper

3. Requires you to come in for cleaning often enough so only a slight amount of plaque is present when you get your teeth cleaned

4. Encourages you to get your teeth straightened no matter how old you are so your teeth will not gradually loosen because they are hitting each other at an angle when you chew

5. Checks and re-cleans any problem areas you may have in your gums after the hygienist has cleaned your teeth

6. Encourages you to replace your silver fillings, as they break down in your molar teeth, with gold or other long lasting material

7. May use a microscope and video display to examine the germs under your gums that cause gum infection, and directs you in a home care and dental office care program that prevents or controls gum disease (gingivitis and periodontitis)

8. Saves teeth with root canal therapy (endodontics) rather than removing teeth

9. Does not allow you to let your gums develop deep pockets and then sends you to a gum specialist friend (periodontist) for expensive gum removal (gingivectomy). (Remember the murdered Long Island periodontist in the movie, *Compromising Positions*; police theorized a suspect might be someone who spent $50,000 and still had bleeding gums)

Summing Up

A quality dentist for adults shows more interest in the health of your gums than in your teeth.

CHAPTER TEN

A CHILD'S VISIT TO THE DENTIST

Dental visits can vary a lot depending on the age of the child, whether there is an obvious problem with the teeth and so forth, but it is worthwhile to discuss what should be done for your child at a routine office visit. The following services do not all have to be done by the dentist personally but some can be done by trained office personnel under the dentist's supervision.

1. ___Fluoride Supplements___. You and your child should be asked about fluoride supplements, drops or tablets, and they should make certain that all the children in the family, not just those being seen by the dentist, have a prescription for fluoride. If the dentist does not help you build strong fluoride teeth but only wants to sell you temporary fluoride treatments, get another dentist. You would not go to a bone specialist who withheld calcium from your children and then sold you plaster casts for their bowed legs. So, why put up with nutritional neglect which is a form of child abuse, from a dentist.

2. ___Diet Instruction and Motivation___. Someone in the office should talk to your children on each visit about their diet, snacks, etc., and instruct and reinforce previous instructions about good eating and drinking habits.

3. ___Home Care___. Someone in the office should instruct the child in how to brush the teeth, how much toothpaste to use and so forth. Older children should be taught to use dental floss and the Water Pik™.

4. ___Examination___. The dentist should do the examination or redo the exam if the child is first seen by a hygienist or an assistant, of all the teeth, the gums, and the bite (occlusion). If all you are told is the child has cavities or has no cavities, and no mention is made of how the teeth are coming into the mouth, whether there is enough room for them to come in straight, and how well the teeth

that are in the mouth are meeting together for chewing, then get another dentist as that office should not be treating children.

5. *X-rays*. Pictures (radiographs) do not need to be taken on each visit but do need to be taken about once a year. One of the benefits of a child having fluoride teeth from taking fluoride supplements in pregnancy and as an infant and child is that we know those teeth rarely have cavities so we do not have to take x-rays every six months. X-rays do have to be taken on all children to look for missing or extra teeth, to check a space for teeth, and for other purposes that are not related to "cavity-checking." The dental office should use high-speed film, a narrow beam (cone), a modern x-ray machine, and a lead apron over the lap when taking x-rays. When these precautions are taken then the amount of radiation involved with a dental film is extremely small, especially when compared with medical x-rays like chest films, etc. With proper technique, a dental x-ray uses the same amount of radiation that you receive by spending a day in Denver, Colorado at 5,000 feet rather than at sea level. One day of skiing at 10,000 feet would be equal to three or four dental films. However, as there is no evidence that x-ray exposure is beneficial, only needed films should be taken. We prefer that the fee for an examination be the same, whether x-rays are taken or not, as we do not think it best for the dental office to have a financial incentive to over-x-radiate.

6. *Cleaning*. The teeth should be cleaned and polished as part of their care and as part of a complete examination as it is difficult to check for cavities if the teeth are dirty. The cleaning can be done with the exam or on a second visit a week or two later.

7. *Fluoride Gel Treatment*. If the dentist has been conscientious about prescribing fluoride supplements to build the mineral into the teeth as they develop, then it is proper that the dentist, once or twice a year, give a fluoride treatment for its additional temporary benefit. The child's head must be tilted down and a

suction used to prevent these highly concentrated gels from being swallowed.

8. ***Communication***. When you leave the dental office you should have a clear understanding of what was done for the child on that visit, what the state of the teeth, gums and bite are, what fluoride supplement was prescribed, when the next appointment is and what is to be done next time. If all you are told is, "we filled one tooth," or "no cavities, come back in 6 months," you are not being recognized as an important part of your child's dental care.

SECTION II
TRAUMA (INJURY)
TO THE MOUTH & TEETH

CHAPTER ELEVEN

PREVENTION AND TREATMENT OF INJURY

Prevention of Injury

Some children fall and hit their teeth; some children fall and skin their knees. If you have the former type child, you will need the services of the dentist, perhaps as early as when the child learns to walk. While we do not advise trying to build an "isolation shelter" there are some tips that are useful for making the home less likely as a cause of accidents. Exposed tile and cement floors should be carpeted. Outdoor carpeting is useful in the patio. Cover the glass cocktail table with a padded cloth during the daytime—it can be removed at night when the children are in bed. Decals on sliding glass doors make good sense and putting tread decals on the bathroom tub or shower if these are slippery should be done. Train your child to look down when they are walking rather than just straight ahead. The new rubber bottom socks seem to help toddlers. Tripping at home and knocking out the front teeth is the main dental accident we see early in life. As the child gets older, we get skateboard, roller skate, bicycle, baseball, soccer, and football injuries as well as the falling out of trees and hitting pool slides, etc. We once catalogued 95 different objects involved in mouth and tooth injuries.

Mouth guards must be worn in contact sports. If possible, use the new clear plastic face guards.

Looks like it is a tooth fairy first down.

Athletics for young children, especially baseball, are a special concern. The child should not be allowed to begin organized sports until he or she is well coordinated enough to reduce the chance of injury. Mouth guards are a must. You can buy them in a sporting goods store or your dentist can make a custom fitted guard for the child. The new full face covering plastic protection shields are much better for baseball than are mouth guards.

Dogs are of concern with small children. Teeth are usually not damaged, but terrible harm can be done to the lips, gums, cheeks, and face. If you have a dog before you have a child, jealousy can result. Older dogs can be testy; young dogs can do damage with a "playful nip." Seek expert advice, but not from the person trying to sell or give you the dog.

Although the injury is usually to the lips, mouth, or throat of the child, not the teeth, childproof your kitchen and bathroom as far as cleaning materials, chemicals and the like. Strong caustics such as lye, sink and drain unstoppers, oven cleaners, and the like should be used when bought and not be in the house at all.

Automobile rides are the most risky activity we engage in. Infant and child seats are a legal requirement now. Children must be trained to use seat belts and not stand on the front seat or floor. Your driving technique, relaxed and defensive, is a more reliable and important training method for your teenagers than just relying on school driving education. Teaching them respect for the mechanical parts of the car can be a more effective motivator for safe driving than lectures and threats about their safety.

Treatment of the Injury—what to do

Injuries can be categorized in terms of their severity.

1. ***In the mildest type,*** there may be lots of blood, some cuts in the mouth, and things may look bad, but if the teeth are not knocked out or not very loose, there should be no great problem. Ice is good treatment. A good ice bag for infants and toddlers is one cube in a Ziploc baggie with a washcloth around it. Place this on the lip gently and hold and comfort the child at the same time. When the bleeding and the child have both calmed down, look inside the mouth and see if the teeth are loose or broken. If the teeth are pushed back up into the gums, they will come back down by themselves, usually in about six weeks. If they are not too loose, just the ice and some aspirin will be sufficient treatment for the time being. The dentist should be told and the child can come in for a check-up at your convenience. Aspirin or Ibuprofen (Advil®, Motrin®) in general are better as they have an anti-inflammatory action and reduce swelling and inflammation, whereas the Tylenol® type products mainly have an effect on temperature, less on pain, and almost no effect on inflammation. If the child has been exposed to chicken pox or has flu-like symptoms, then Tylenol® should be used, of course.

2. ***Tooth is extremely loose.*** This requires a visit to the dentist immediately. The dentist will take an x-ray to see if the root is broken and may need to splint or wire the loose tooth to the ones

next to it so that it will not come out and so that the socket can harden around it. Often a liquid antibiotic for four or five days is useful in helping these injuries heal.

3. ***Teeth are broken.*** If one or more teeth are broken or fractured, then the tooth should be x-rayed to see the extent of the injury and make sure the root is not injured. If the break does not involve the pulp or the nerve, then the dentist can either smooth it if it is a small break, or can use a bonding technique to rebuild the tooth if there is a large segment missing, especially on permanent teeth. Bonding to recreate the broken piece of the tooth is painless but requires 15 to 30 minutes for the procedure and for the material to set, so the child does have to be able to cooperate for that time. If the tooth is bonded then no brown soda pop should be drunk as these contain phosphoric acid which stains the bonded teeth and dissolves the bonding material.

4. ***A more severe injury with tooth knocked out of the mouth.*** In this case, the tooth should be recovered, rinsed off with tap water, quickly put back into the socket, and held there with clean gauze or a Kleenex™. The only time the parent should not attempt to replant the tooth is if it is a baby tooth with its root broken, or with a root that is very short because it is almost time to lose the tooth anyway. If the parent cannot replant the tooth, it should be placed in milk and transported to the dentist's office as an emergency. Normally it is best to get these back in the mouth within 20 minutes as the longer they are out, the less satisfactory the result. Sometimes a root canal has to be done on these teeth, but not always. It is important to check these teeth at intervals for several years because they will have some root resorption and may be lost no matter how skillful the treatment. The majority, however, can be saved if treatment is rapid and we have many patients who have a permanent tooth that was knocked out when they were 9 or 10 years of age and still have those teeth more than 20 years later.

5. ***Delayed tooth reaction to injury.*** All mouths and teeth that have been involved in injury should be checked periodically by the parent by looking inside the mouth to observe the color of the back (the tongue side) of the tooth. If the color is changing from normal pale white or yellow and is becoming gray or even black, then the dentist should be consulted. The nerve can be slowly dying from the injury, and root canal treatment may be needed in either a baby tooth or a permanent tooth. Sometimes a tooth will turn dark soon after the injury due to bleeding into the pulp or nerve like a "black eye," but the nerve may not die and this can gradually clear and the tooth will regain a more normal color without root canal therapy. In general, about 75 percent of blackened teeth will need pulp or root canal therapy if they are primary baby teeth. Almost all darkened permanent teeth need root canal treatment, but in any case, an observation period of at least several weeks is indicated rather than rushing to do immediate root canal therapy. An injured tooth which develops an infected area in the bone, and which may show a "pimple" on the gum above the tooth, is abscessed and does require root canal therapy. An infected baby tooth with extensive root resorption or a baby tooth that was about ready to fall out anyway would be removed by the dentist rather than be treated with a root canal.

Eat your lunch right now, Jason!

O.K., but my first bite will not be from my plate!

At 12:32 PM, JR, age 4, was told by his mother to eat his lunch. As she turned away, JR bit her blue jean clad rear end. His upper incisor caught on a copper rivet and pulled out the tooth, not the rivet. His mother rinsed off the tooth, placed it back in its socket at 12:37 PM, and was in our office to have it splinted in place at 1:00 PM. The blue jean copper rivet made number 96 on our tooth injury list.

SECTION III
ORTHODONTICS

Maybe snaggle tooth isn't such a good nickname?

CHAPTER TWELVE

PREVENTION

In order to tell you about preventing or lessening the need for orthodontics, we must review what we know about the causes of crooked teeth.

Causes of Crooked Teeth that Require Orthodontics

1. *Heredity.* The size of our baby teeth and permanent teeth, and the shape of our jaws, how wide and how long they are, are controlled by heredity just as is the shape of various parts of our body, the color of our hair, and so forth. A problem occurs when a child inherits the father's large upper jaw and perhaps the mother's smaller lower jaw or the child inherits the father's narrow jaw and the mother's wide teeth. This type of mismatching probably occurs more often in a melting pot society such as the United States, where longheaded people marry round headed people and so forth. There is probably less of this in a more homogeneous population where most of the people have similar shapes to their faces and jaws.

2. *Too many teeth for the mouth.* The normal number of thirty-two permanent teeth are, for many people, too many for our less wide or long, less prominent jaws that people tend to have now as compared to 100,000 years ago, or 6,011 years ago, depending on your point of view. However, we continue, in general, to have the same number of teeth, although more and more people find that they are congenitally missing the wisdom teeth which does help solve that problem. The point is that many mouths are crowded because there is just not room for 32 teeth in the jaws of most Caucasian people these days.

3. *Tongue habits.* It is thought that infants, who are bottle-fed, especially with a wide-open type nipple so that the child can be fed more rapidly, develop a habit of controlling the flow of milk

or formula with the tongue in the front of their mouth. Thus the child learns to swallow with what is known as a tongue thrust or a forward pushing of the tongue which tends to cause the teeth, especially those of the upper jaw, to be pushed forward of their normal positions.

4. ***Airway problems-breathing obstruction.*** Another cause of crooked teeth is due to early breathing problems during childhood. If a child, due to extremely large adenoids and/or nasal allergies, must breathe through his mouth most of the time then the child might develop what is known as adenoid face, which means that the mouth is open, the lower jaw drops back, the tongue is forward and the palate tends to be high and narrow.

5. ***Thumb sucking.*** A child, who is a particularly determined thumb sucker and tends to suck the thumb in a very forceful way most of the day and past the normal age of 2 to 3 years, will often cause or at least aggravate any tendencies for protrusion of the upper jaw that may be present.

6. ***Missing or extra teeth.*** If there are extra teeth blocking the path of the normal teeth or if there are missing teeth then this will interfere with the normal order of the teeth in the mouth and produce an abnormal bite (occlusion).

PREVENTION

1. *Heredity.* There is not much we are going to do about this. Most people are not going to choose their mates on the basis of their dental arches. Before we knew how to perfect teeth with fluoride, people used to say it would be better to check out the prospective mate's teeth rather than the color of their eyes, but now that we can overcome a tendency toward "soft teeth" with fluoride, this is no longer true. The most we can expect from heredity is to observe each side of the family and be prepared to try to intercept or treat at an early age the inevitable orthodontic problem, so that it will not become severe and require more extensive treatment during the teen years.

2. *Tongue thrust* can be prevented by using modern type nipples on baby bottles and not using a hot needle or other object to enlarge the opening so the child can feed more rapidly. Also, the children should be fed sitting up rather than lying down, so that they do not have to use their tongue to keep too much formula from going into their throat. The child should feed more slowly and avoid gulping the milk.

3. *Airway problems* should be observed. It can be normal for many children at age 18 months to 3 years to be somewhat adenoidal, that is, to have somewhat enlarged adenoids and to snore a bit, especially when they have a cold. If they are in daycare or nursery, they may have colds and other viruses almost continuously for the first two years. However, if the child is a snoring, heavy breather, even when well, then the child should be checked by an ear, nose and throat surgeon to evaluate the possible desirability of having adenoids and/or tonsils removed and/or some allergic treatment. There is increasing awareness in the dental and medical professions that blockage of the breathing passage in the nose and between the nose and the throat (the nasopharynx) in early childhood can have an unfortunate effect on the growth and development of the upper and lower jaws. Difficulty in breathing through the nose seems to be associated with a high narrow palate, crowding

of the teeth, and a long, narrow face. Early correction of the breathing problem, often associated with interceptive orthodontic treatment, can improve the outlook for many of these children. Sixty percent of the growth of the face is complete by age four, and ninety percent by age twelve when traditional orthodontics often begins. It is far easier for the child and the dentist, and we can usually get a better final result, if some of these problems are corrected before the face and jaws are fully-grown.*

---

* Our interest in the dental complications resulting from early airway problems has been motivated, in part, by the work of the late William McTavish, D.D.S., of Houston, and George Meredith, M.D., of Norfolk.

CHAPTER THIRTEEN

PREVENTIVE ORTHODONTIC TREATMENT

General Considerations: There are several conditions that you and your children's dentist should look for as the baby teeth and permanent teeth appear in the mouth. These conditions can be corrected in a simple manner if they are noticed when they first appear, but can cause severe, costly problems if neglected.

1. *Crossbite*. The upper jaw teeth slightly overlap the bottom jaw teeth in the normal bite or occlusion. You already know that this is true for the front teeth but may not know that the same is also true for the molars in the rear of the mouth.

   Look in your or your child's mouth by holding the cheek out with your finger or a spoon handle and have the child bite down as in normal chewing and see if the cheek side of all the upper teeth are slightly wider or slightly outside of the lower teeth. If any of the lower teeth are outside of the upper teeth, then that is a crossbite and it needs to be corrected. There are two general types of crossbite.

   a. *Simple Crossbite*. One or two front teeth are out of line—such as the cuspid (eyetooth) or front incisor. This can often be corrected at age 2½ - 3 by smoothing off the tip of the lower jaw tooth that is pointed and locked outside the corresponding upper jaw tooth. After your dentist does this painless procedure, the upper jaw tooth will gradually move out over the lower tooth in about six months time.

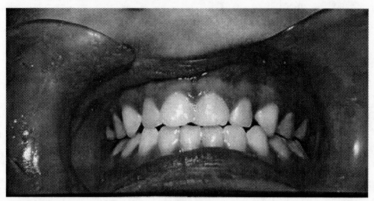

The patient's left lateral incisor (seen on the right side of the picture) is slightly inside the lower incisor [Illustration of a simple crossbite.]

b. ***Severe Crossbite*** can occur by age three when all the teeth from the cuspid (eyetooth) on back, including the two baby molars are out of line—that is, the lower jaw teeth are outside of the upper teeth. This condition can exist on only one side of the mouth (unilateral crossbite), or on both sides (bilateral crossbite). These conditions are best treated in the young child, age 4-6 years, by a rapid palatal expander appliance. It is cemented to the upper teeth like a fixed retainer and the key in the center is turned by the parent once or twice a day and the upper molars are pushed out wider and into the normal position. As the name implies, depending upon the child and parent's cooperation, the correction can be accomplished in as little as ten to twelve weeks. See diagram picture on next page.

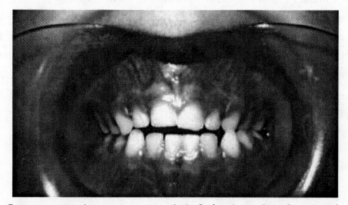

Severe cross bite on patient's left (right side of picture).

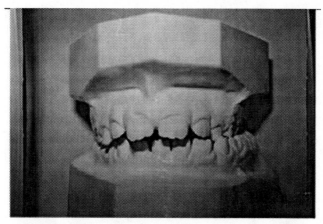

Severe cross bite on patient's left—four upper teeth inside the lower.

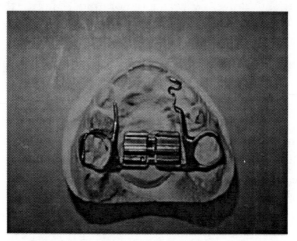

Rapid palatal expander (RPE) appliance.

2. **_Extra tooth._** One percent (1 out of 100) of children will have one or more extra teeth. If it is a baby tooth, it is usually removed at the time the permanent tooth is due to appear. If it is a permanent extra tooth, it must also be removed but the timing of the removal varies depending on the location as it must be removed when it will give the least risk of damaging the normal tooth developing next to it.

3. **_Missing teeth._** Five to six percent (1 out of 20) of children are born missing one or more teeth. This is called ***congenitally***

missing tooth **or** *teeth* and the tendency to this condition can run in a family.

a. ***Congenitally missing primary (baby) tooth or teeth.*** This is rare, but if there is a congenitally missing primary (baby) tooth then the same permanent tooth above it is also missing as the permanent teeth develop from the remnant of the primary teeth. A small bridge may be needed to keep the space open and keep the other teeth from drifting.

b. ***Congenitally missing permanent tooth or teeth.*** One in twenty children will have this condition and it can be diagnosed, for the front teeth and first permanent molars, with 97 percent accuracy, at age 3½ with a panoramic (panorex) x-ray. It can be diagnosed with the same accuracy for the rear cuspid, premolar, and second molar teeth by age 5½ by a panoramic x-ray. This is why quality dentists do this x-ray starting at age 3 to 4 and then every 3 years during childhood.

   The lower permanent second bicuspid (premolar) tooth is the most frequently missing, other than the wisdom teeth. This tooth comes into the mouth at age 11, replacing the second baby molar, right in front of the first permanent (six year) molar. Sometimes the baby molar can be kept as a permanent tooth but as the roots of the baby teeth usually will not allow the tooth to last a lifetime, it is usually better to shift the permanent molar teeth forward to fill in the gap.

   In the case of a missing lateral incisor (smallest front tooth), sometimes the cuspid (eye) tooth can be moved over and reshaped to look like the missing incisor. This is usually preferable to having a bridge made in the case of permanent teeth.

4. ***Crowding of the front teeth.*** Like a crossbite, this is a problem you can diagnose. There is usually room for primary (baby) teeth but often the jaw is not yet big enough for the larger permanent teeth

when they appear in the front of the mouth. Instead of letting the permanent teeth get fixed in the jaw in a crooked fashion and then needing major orthodontics as a teenager, a quality dentist will make the effort to trim the side or sides of the baby tooth next to the permanent tooth that is trying to fit into the space. In at least 80 percent of the children that are having crowding of the front permanent teeth as they appear, this simple technique will provide enough space to allow the permanent teeth to fit correctly into the jaw. This is called *disking* or *serial reduction of the baby teeth.* It works because as we gradually go back in the mouth, trimming each baby tooth in turn as each permanent tooth comes in, we get to the primary (baby) molars that are larger than the permanent teeth that replace them at age 9 to 12. These are the bicuspids (premolars) which are the only permanent teeth that are smaller than the primary teeth they replace. Therefore, we finally regain the space that we have been borrowing, tooth by tooth, starting in the front of the mouth at age six.

If we remove the baby teeth instead of disking them, the back molar teeth will simply move forward and make the crowding even worse. **We know this looks complicated, but read the previous paragraph again and look at the diagram until you understand it. Important!**

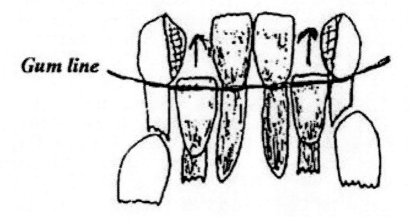

Illustration of disking or serial reduction technique authored by Dr. William Wyatt, Hurst, TX.

The shaded two center teeth are the two permanent lower central incisors that are already in. The teeth on each side of them are the two lateral incisors that are being forced to come in crooked as the space with the arrows is not quite wide enough. Your dentist disks off the sides of the baby teeth (the crosshatched area) to gain the needed space and the lower permanent front teeth do not get fixed in a twisted, crowded position. The same disking can be done to the baby molars to help the permanent bicuspids come in straight. This is what dentists should be doing for children rather than drilling and filling cavities they shouldn't have.

In about 15 percent of children with crowding, the disking technique does not create enough space, and the teeth eventually must be removed. These children usually must have their four first permanent bicuspids (premolar) teeth removed (bicuspid extractions). Neither primary nor permanent teeth should be removed for orthodontic reasons, unless the dentist is capable of doing full orthodontic treatment and first has done study models (plaster casts of the jaws) and cephalometric x-rays (side view and front view of the whole head) so the dentist can measure the jaws and skull growth points and try to predict the amount and direction of the jaw growth that will occur. If at all possible, the orthodontics should be finished without removing any permanent teeth, except for the wisdom teeth (third permanent molars). (Chapter 19, Error II.)

5. ***Retained primary (baby) teeth.*** Twenty percent (1 in 5) of children will have a primary tooth try to stay in the mouth instead of falling out when it should. The permanent tooth will then try to come in back or in front of the baby tooth. As one little patient said, "It's like two cars are in one parking spot." This condition requires immediate removal of the baby tooth.

6. ***Delayed eruption of a permanent tooth.*** Twenty percent (1 in 5) of children will need help getting a permanent tooth through the gums—most often the upper central incisors. This is due to an unusually thick, tough gum tissue. If a permanent tooth does not come in within six months after the primary (baby) tooth has fallen out, it should be checked. With a little local anesthetic on and in the gum, a piece of tissue is removed to uncover the tooth and let it come in. Since your quality dentist obtained a panoramic x-ray at age three and six, we know the tooth is not missing!

7. ***Premature loss of primary (baby) tooth.*** If a baby tooth is lost before it is supposed to fall out—knocked out with an injury or if a non-fluoride baby molar is lost because of decay and the permanent tooth is not due to appear for a year or more, then a space maintainer should be put in. This is especially critical for baby molars—if they are not replaced by a space maintainer, then the first permanent molar (six-year molar) will drift forward, and block out the space in which the permanent bicuspids (premolars) are due to appear at age 11 or 12.

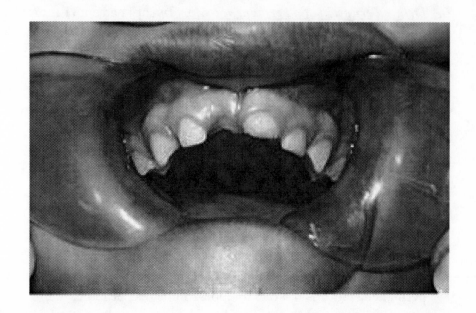

Before

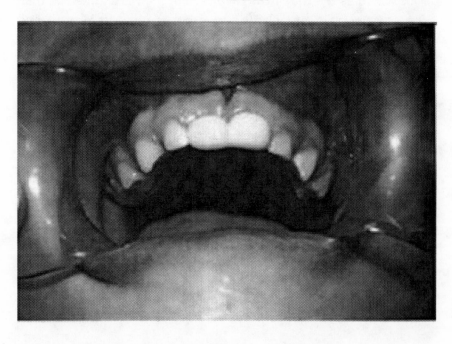

Space maintainer for front tooth in place.

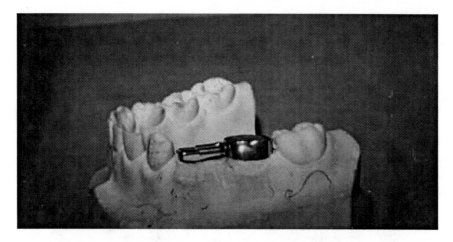

Space maintainers for a baby molar.

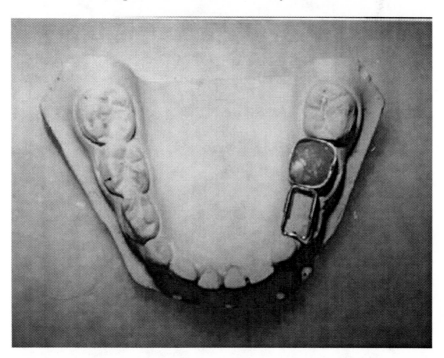

8. ***Open bite***. This means that the front teeth are apart or open when the rear teeth (the molars) are together when the child bites down or chews. It is caused by heredity, tongue thrust, airway problems, and prolonged abnormal thumb sucking. If there is an open bite in the baby teeth, your dentist can work with the child

or help stop the tongue thrust or abnormal thumb sucking habit. With an open bite in the permanent teeth, it must be corrected with full orthodontic treatment (see next chapter).

Illustration of an open bite starting treatment.

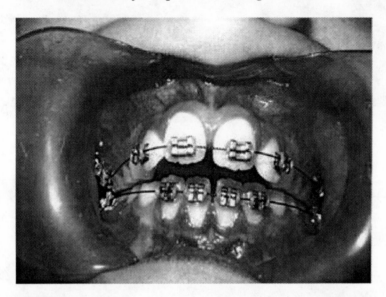

Open bite corrected with a little straight wire orthodontics.

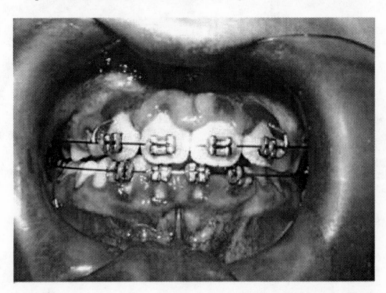

9. ***Protrusion of the upper front teeth—overjet—best known as "buck teeth."*** Overjet may be combined with an open bite. There are two types of overbite or overjet. *Class I*—the molars are in correct position with each other, but the front teeth stick out. *Class II*—the upper molars are forward of their normal position, with or without the front teeth sticking out. These two abnormal bites or occlusions have the same causes as the open bite. If an overjet or overbite exists, it should be corrected orthodontically as soon as the child can be motivated to cooperate, usually between ages six to eight years.

   If the permanent teeth are protruding (if the child has "buck teeth"), they should be pulled back into position as soon as all four upper incisors (front teeth) are in the mouth. Orthodontic treatment is required, i.e. bands and brackets on the permanent teeth and an arch wire. The treatment takes six to nine months and then an upper retainer is worn twenty-four hours a day for six months and then only at night for an additional six months. ***Buckteeth should be corrected at this early age; they never should be left until the child is 12 or 14 years old for two very important reasons.***

   a. The teeth are too easily injured and get broken or knocked out.

   b. The child looks strange during the years from age 6 to 12 in which his or her self-image is forming (see next chapter). Allowing a child's front teeth to protrude until they are 12 or more years old is an act of cruelty and is not to be tolerated in any civilized society.

CHAPTER FOURTEEN

INTERCEPTIVE ORTHODONTICS (EARLY ORTHODONTIC REATMENT: PHASE I)

Years ago, it was traditional to allow all the permanent teeth to come into the mouth before any orthodontic treatment was done, usually beginning at age 12 to 14. Now we know that 80 percent of children with an orthodontic problem should be treated between the ages of six and ten. Early treatment is desirable because:

1. The teeth do not get a chance to become fixed in the jawbone in an abnormal position.

2. We get to take advantage of the rapid growth in the jaws during ages six to ten which make it easier to place the teeth in the proper position.

3. It protects the teeth against injury.

4. Children are often more cooperative at this age than as teenagers.

5. Treatment time is short; six to nine months.

Simple preventive orthodontics such as correction of a crossbite, etc., can usually be done on the basis of normal dental records; that is, examination and panoramic x-rays. Before starting any treatment of a more complicated orthodontic problem, however, full orthodontic records must be made. These consist of examination, panoramic x-ray, plaster casts of the upper and lower teeth (study models), and a cephalogram (growth plate x-rays of the head with a side and front view). These records are analyzed and a plan is made for placing the teeth into as normal position as possible in your child. At this time, you should have a conference with your dentist and be given a clear understanding of expected treatment time, cost, and whether permanent teeth (the bicuspids) will have to be removed. Eight out of ten children needing orthodontics can be treated without removing permanent teeth other than the wisdom teeth. About 15 percent of children needing orthodontics simply will not have enough room for 28 teeth and must end up with 24 permanent teeth in the mouth. An orthodontic plan that involves removal of the permanent bicuspid teeth should be done with great care and possibly with second opinion consultation so that your child does not risk ending up with one of the most common errors in orthodontics results, a flat face (see Chapter 19).

What orthodontic problem should be treated early, that is, before all the permanent teeth are in the mouth? **The orthodontic problems that should be treated early are:**

1. Buck teeth

2. Crossbite

3. Open bite

4. Any severe bite problem that endangers the teeth and/or the gums and cheeks.

Does early treatment avoid the need for treatment at age 12 to 14? Not usually, strongas most children who have early treatment will need a short final treatment phase of 9-12 months after all the permanent teeth are in the mouth. The early treatment phase of 6-9 months at age 6 to 10 and the final treatment phase of 9-12 months at age 12 to 14 do not exceed the total time usually needed for traditional one stage treatment during the teen years. The cost is about the same and we have the five advantages listed at the start of this chapter.

Who does not require early treatment? Children who do not have to have early treatment but can wait and have their orthodontics done at one 18-month long treatment session as a teen, when all the baby teeth have been shed and all the 12-year molars are in are those with the following conditions:

1. Children with mild, slight bite (occlusion) problems

2. Those children with an emotional problem or who are significantly retarded and children who are not mature enough emotionally to be treated or to cooperate with treatment at 6 to 10

3. Children, especially boys, who cannot be motivated to cooperate with the treatment as a pre-teen

4. Late developers: children (more boys than girls) who do not shed the last of their primary teeth until age 12 years or later. The "dental age" of the patient may be younger than the child's chronological or real age. There are very bright children who are slow tooth shedders.

CHAPTER FIFTEEN

REMOVABLE ORTHODONTIC APPLIANCES (FUNCTIONALS)

Appliances that look like large retainers and are removable, that is, not cemented to the teeth, are called *functionals*. These were largely developed in Europe, and now are used in this country, usually for interceptive early treatment. They are promoted on the basis of the advantages of early interceptive treatment given in the last chapter. However, functionals should not be sold on the basis of the advantages of early orthodontic treatment, but should be compared with early orthodontic treatment using fixed, regular braces.

The disadvantages of functionals are:

1. Must be worn a long time—usually two years or more to accomplish less than can be done with fixed braces in 6 months. This can tire the child and turn him off to orthodontics.

2. They are often used by dentists who are just learning orthodontics as all the dentist must do is to make casts of the child's jaws and send them to the appliance company which makes the device.

3. The long time they must be worn can lead to unnecessary expense and they can serve as a "financial arch-wire" (See Chapter 19).

4. They get lost and broken—sometimes on purpose—for which I can not always blame the child as she/he is expected to spend most of his/her childhood with a cross between a retainer and a denture in his mouth.

5. They may not do much.

The advantages of functional removable appliances are:

1. There is a possibility that they stimulate some growth in the jaw. However, as they are worn for long periods of time during which all children's jaws grow, the dentist may be taking credit and getting paid for something that is going to happen anyway.

2. It is more difficult to do harm with them. Since functionals do not have the regular, strong forces of fixed braces, if the dentist is inexperienced in orthodontics, he can rationalize by saying, "I may not be doing much good, but at least I won't do much harm."

3. They are removed daily and this allows better cleaning of the teeth.

We find it better to use the orthodontic forces and more precise control over each tooth that braces give us so we can get in and straighten the teeth in 6 to 9 months and get finished. Functionals seem to be used more in small towns and rural areas where children will do as they are told—no matter how long it takes.

The first reason often given for using functionals concerns number three above—dental hygiene. With our fluoride sufficient teeth that have such effective decay prevention built in the teeth, we do not find this to be a valid reason for using functionals.

CHAPTER SIXTEEN

FINAL AND/OR FULL ORTHODONTIC TREATMENT

Final and/or full orthodontic treatment is done when nearly all the baby teeth have been shed or are about to be shed and the 12-year molars are in or about to come in. Orthodontic records must be made: panoramic x-ray, plaster casts (study model), and cephalogram (cephalometric front and side view head x-rays). You must have a conference with the dentist and be told the diagnosis, treatment plan, time of treatment, and cost. If the dentist says that the four permanent bicuspid teeth must be removed, and if you can see that there is severe crowding with large teeth and a small jaw, and the dentist meets the standards outlined in Chapter 17, you may proceed. If the need for losing the permanent teeth is borderline or if you have any doubt, get a second opinion. If your dentist uses something other than the straight wire technique and advises permanent tooth removal, get a second opinion from a dentist who uses a straight wire method. It is much better to finish orthodontic treatment in a 14 year old with the teeth slightly full with just a bit of the "Julia Roberts" look, rather than perfectly straight and flat, because by the time the child is 18 or 20 and their head and face has grown some and filled out, they can have a pinched look to their mouth with a rather flat profile (see Chapter 19).

You should know your dentist's qualifications for delivering quality orthodontics, the technique he or she uses, and the final goals of treatment (see Chapter 19 & 20). Full orthodontic treatment is done with metal bands around the molar teeth, bonded (cemented) small brackets on the rest of the teeth, an arch wire connecting all the teeth of each jaw, using elastic bands between the braces on each jaw, and occasionally headgear—an elastic band around the back of the head to pull the rear molars back in the jaw.

Because of their importance, the questions of who should do your child's orthodontics, how long should it take and cost, what is a quality result, what techniques are best, what are the major errors, and how they can be avoided are discussed separately in the following chapters.

CHAPTER SEVENTEEN

WHO DOES ORTHODONTICS?

Orthodontics is the movement of the teeth. Any dentist who treats children should be able to do the simple tooth movements discussed in Chapters 13 and 14 on preventive and interceptive orthodontics. If the dentist is only a cavity checker and tooth cleaner, he is not a quality dentist for a child.

A quality dentist does not have to be qualified to perform full orthodontic treatment. Who, then, should do your child's orthodontics?

1. ***Pediatric dentist.*** Of those children's dentists who are qualified to do full orthodontics, most are members of the American Orthodontic Society (AOS) of Dallas, Texas and should be Board eligible or Board certified by that organization.

American Orthodontic Society (AOS)
11884 Greenville Avenue, Suite 112
Dallas, Texas 75243
Telephone: 1-800-448-1601
Web site: www.orthodontics.com

The International Association of Orthodontics (IAO), its sister organization, certifies similar qualifications and works largely in Canada, overseas, as well as, in the US, in Milwaukee, Wisconsin, are acceptable.

International Association of Orthodontics (IAO)
750 North Lincoln Memorial Drive, Suite 422
Milwaukee, Wisconsin 53202
Telephone: 1-800-447-8770
Web site: www.iaortho.org

Pediatric dentists have a natural interest in keeping the teeth free of cavities so they often will get the orthodontics done faster so that the food catching braces are not on longer than absolutely necessary. Since the pediatric dentists also will be doing twice a year cleanings and checkups and may remove the wisdom teeth (third molars) when the orthodontics is completed, they can usually charge less for the orthodontics than can a dentist who does nothing but orthodontics. There is also an advantage to having one person (beside yourself and the child) responsible for the final quality of the teeth at age 18. When two dentists are involved and the final occlusion is not as it should be (see Chapter 20—The Ideal Orthodontic Result), then there may be a tendency for the orthodontist to say that he or she did not get to see the child at a young enough age, etc., and the regular dentist will say that he or she guesses that the orthodontist did what he could, etc.

However, do not be bashful about asking your dentist about his or her qualifications in orthodontics. You can also contact the appropriate certifying organization.

2. ***General dentist (family dentist).*** Some general dentists are also qualified in orthodontics. A few are so talented that they limit their practices to nothing but orthodontics. There are general dentists/orthodontists in California, Texas, and Oklahoma, for example, who are largely responsible for developing our most modern method of doing orthodontics, The Straight Wire Technique. As with the pediatric dentist, family dentists who are qualified in orthodontics belong to the American Orthodontic Society (AOS), or the International Association of Orthodontic (IAO).

3. ***Orthodontists.*** Dentists who call themselves orthodontists usually have gone straight from dental school into a one or two year training program in orthodontics and then have done only orthodontics in their practice. Some like a well-known orthodontist just south of San Francisco, use and helped develop modern techniques and are recognized for doing excellent work.

Unfortunately, in many areas "the best orthodontist in town" can be an older dentist who uses obsolete methods, takes three years or more to do 18 months work, runs an assembly line practice, and is satisfied with mediocre results. (See Chapter 20—The Ideal Orthodontic Result). These dentists belong to the American Association of Orthodontics of Chicago, Illinois and should be Board certified, or at least Board eligible as determined by that organization. (Tel. 1-800- 424-2841)

4. ***Oral surgeons***. Jaw surgery (Orthognathic surgery) is sometimes needed for orthodontic purposes. This is done by an oral surgeon. For children, it is sometimes required to reduce a long lower jaw (Class III malocclusion) and for adults, it is used to obtain major orthodontic change very rapidly. These dentists are certified by the American Association of Oral and Maxillofacial Surgeons of Chicago, Illinois.

CHAPTER EIGHTEEN

THE COST OF ORTHODONTICS

Fees differ in various parts of the country so it is more difficult to tell you what orthodontics should cost in your town. At the present time, the year 2007, in Florida, full orthodontics cost about $2,500 to $3,500. The treatment should take about 18 months and occasionally up to 2 years. This is active treatment time and does not include the time spent wearing retainers, usually an additional year. The cost of not having orthodontics done is much more than going through life with a less than ideal smile. The true cost is unnecessary loss of teeth due to stress being placed on them because they meet at odd angles when chewing. Also, problems with the jaw joints (temporomandibular joint or TMJ) are more likely when teeth are left with a malocclusion (uneven bite).

CHAPTER NINETEEN

THE MOST COMMON ERRORS IN ORTHODONTICS AND HOW TO AVOID THEM

Error I—The Financial Archwire

A dental archwire is the name for braces—the wire that connects the teeth in orthodontic treatment. This is known as a financial archwire when the braces are mostly producing income for the dentist, rather than results for the patient. There are two ways that this can happen:

A. *Holding archwire.* A dentist may put on braces for a year or more after the front permanent teeth and/or the first permanent molars are in the mouth. The archwire is adjusted so that it does not do much and is on a "holding pattern." A dentist may do this so as to "brand" the patient as his. Once he puts braces on no other dentist can do the orthodontics unless you discharge the first dentist. The holding archwire also lengthens the treatment time about one year and therefore justifies a larger fee. We are not talking about braces that are put on at ages 6-10 as discussed in Chapter 14, Interceptive Orthodontics. In that case the braces are put on for 6-9 months for a specific purpose and the teeth are quickly moved and straightened. For the holding archwire, you are told it is time for braces but are only given a vague explanation of what is to be accomplished in the first 6-12 months.

B. *Excessive treatment time.* The second type of financial archwire is found in a 3 to 5 year treatment plan. Here the dentist puts on the braces correctly at the proper time but then manages to take 3 to 5 years to do 18 months work. When doing orthodontics on preteens and teenagers, if a dentist does not complete most of his or her patients in 18 months, or takes more than 2 years on the occasional complex patient, then the dentist is either using an old fashioned, obsolete method, is not certain about what he or she is doing, or is taking longer than necessary in order to justify the fee. These treatment times are for active treatment and do not include the time needed for retainers. Adult orthodontics usually takes longer as the teeth and bones are harder to move, as the bones are not growing.

How to avoid a financial archwire? Use the knowledge you have gained from this book and insist on a clear understanding of what it is the dentist will do and why, and what will be the time of treatment and the cost, include the time for retainers, and assume that you and the child cooperate fully with the dentist. If you have any doubts, get a consultation with a dentist who uses a modern method such as the Straight Wire Technique that allows more consistent rapid straightening of the teeth.

Error II—The Flat Face (Eighteen Wheeler Syndrome or Long Dark Corridors Syndrome)

A flat or dished in face often results if the permanent teeth, the bicuspids, are removed for orthodontics when it is not absolutely necessary. Some of the old orthodontic techniques work best with extracting these teeth and it is sometimes done just to make it easier for the dentist to do the orthodontics rather than because it is absolutely necessary for the benefit of the patient. Some of these children look all right when their orthodontics are finished at age 14 or 15, but when the child gets his or her full facial growth at age 18 or 20, he or she may have a flat dished in profile and a narrow pinched look in the mouth on front view. Saying that they look as if they had been run over by an eighteen-wheeler truck is an unkind but apt description. This look is now better named the *Long Dark Corridors Syndrome* because as they smile, you see dark spaces between the teeth and the cheeks.

An example of the appearance of an adult when permanent bicuspids are removed for orthodontics as a teenager when it is not absolutely necessary. The child may look fine when this is done at 14 to 16 years of age, but when fully grown, the part of the face between the nose and the chin looks narrow, constricted, and dished in. When smiling, there is a long dark corridor to each side of the teeth. Focus groups rate persons with this defect as less trustworthy than persons with a wide set of teeth. No wonder McCain and Bush won in NH and Forbes had to withdraw from the 2000 presidential race.

How to avoid a flat face? Use a dentist who uses a modern technique that does not require unnecessary bicuspid removal and who doesn't run an orthodontic mill whereby bicuspids are removed for the convenience of the office rather than for the need of the patient. Remember that about 15 percent of children (1 in 6) who require full orthodontics do need their bicuspids out. These children usually have the worst crowding, with large, wider than normal incisors, and just have no room for 28 permanent teeth. Five to ten percent of children are borderline with the measurements on their cephalogram indicating that the teeth will be tight but all the permanent teeth, except for the wisdom teeth, could be fitted in. In these cases, insist that your child be finished with the bicuspids in, even if it results in a slightly full, almost "Julia Roberts look." This will look a lot better when the child is grown.

Nearly all children who require orthodontics need to have their wisdom teeth removed, but this does not cause any flattening of the face as they are in the rear of the jaws.

Error III—The Gummy Smile

This common error is easy to spot. When the person smiles, instead of just seeing the teeth, you see part or all of the upper gums. This look is frequently found after orthodontic treatment with older techniques such as Labial-Lingual, Begg, and Edgewise. These techniques make it difficult to torque or twist the roots of the teeth back into the mouth rather than just pulling in the crown or the visible part of the teeth. These techniques also make it difficult for the dentist to intrude the teeth up into the jaw. There are a few people whose upper lip is so short that they will have somewhat of a gummy smile no matter what technique or how skilled the dentist. Cosmetic surgery and cosmetic gum trimming are available for these few persons.

Ms. Lewinsky has a moderately gummy smile. That is all we probably should say about that. You can see more severe cases if you look around. How to avoid the gummy smile? Use the Straight Wire Technique and a quality dentist.

Error IV—The Deep Bite

If the upper teeth overlap the lower teeth too much—more than 1-3 mm—then the distance from the nose to the chin is shortened and that is termed a deep bite or a failure to open the bite. This often comes with Error II—The Flat Face, as a result of removing bicuspids when it is not absolutely necessary. Besides avoiding unnecessary bicuspid removal, your dentist can avoid this common error by extruding (lengthening) the molars and intruding (pushing up into the jaw) the incisors. These maneuvers are more easily done with the Straight Wire Technique.

Error V—Failure to Remove Wisdom Teeth (3rd molars)

When the orthodontics is completed, the wisdom teeth should be removed before they erupt into the mouth. Otherwise they push the rest of the teeth forward and crowd the front teeth, especially in the lower jaw. Removing the wisdom teeth at the proper time is as important for keeping a good orthodontic result as is wearing a retainer. (See Chapter 23, Wisdom Teeth and Why It is Smart to Remove Them in Your Mid-Teens).

Error VI—Open Spaces

Visible spaces should not be left between teeth. Too often, after bicuspids have been removed, spaces are left behind the cuspid (eyetooth). Care must be taken to pull all the teeth together. Open spaces occur with the unnecessary removal of bicuspids and seem to be more of a problem with the Begg technique.

Error VII—Rotated Teeth

Individual teeth should not be left rotated. The chewing edge of the teeth should be correctly aligned. In order to achieve this as an end result, a tooth may have to be overcorrected as there is a tendency for it to try to return to its original position. Also, doing the orthodontics as young as possible helps to prevent rotated teeth, as they do not have as much time to get fixed in a crooked position in the jaw. If there is a relapse, orthodontic retreatment and/or a fibrotomy (cutting the elastic fiber between the tooth and the socket which can cause the tooth to return to the original crooked or rotated position) may be necessary. The longer a tooth stays rotated, the easier it is for it to return to that position—another reason for early treatment.

Error VIII—Horse Teeth or the Bugs Bunny Syndrome

This error often occurs in children who have narrow faces and mouths. The dentist pulls the upper front teeth back with the braces but fails to push the teeth up into the jaw. As a result, the center incisor teeth are left too long. This error can usually be avoided by using a technique that permits the dentist to intrude or push the teeth up into the jaw in order to shorten the teeth and avoid a horsey look. This maneuver is most easily done with the Straight Wire Technique.

Error IX—Failure to Remove Bicuspids When Necessary (Bimaxillary Protrusion)

In contrast to Error II, the flat face which can result from ill advised removal of the permanent bicuspids (premolars), these teeth need to be removed in about 15 percent of children who need full orthodontics. If these teeth are not removed, the front teeth will tend to push forward and overlap after orthodontic treatment is finished. Besides the dental measurements and projections of expected jaw growth, the parents and the dentist need to look at the child's face—especially the mid-face—the portion formed by the upper jaw. If the mid-face is too full and both upper and lower teeth protrude markedly, then it is usually safer to remove four bicuspids if the dental situation seems to require it. If the middle part of the child's face is weak, flat, or narrow, you may decide to keep the bicuspids. Black children more frequently require the removal of these teeth than do white children. The important point is that you and your dentist must consider the child's face, not just the teeth.

Error X—Failure To Level the Smile Line

The smile line is an imaginary line drawn along the biting edges of the upper teeth from cuspid (eyetooth) to cuspid (eyetooth). It is the line of the teeth that is seen when a person smiles. The biting edges of the four upper front teeth (incisors) should be almost in a flat straight line. The central two incisors can be very slightly longer than the lateral incisors and then the cuspids (eyetooth) again slightly longer in order to protect the occlusion (bite). A common error is to have the central incisors too long with each next tooth being higher and higher. This is called "the stairway to the stars" since the teeth look like the white stairs they used to have in the Hollywood musicals of the 1930s and 1940s.

Error XI—Failure To Avoid Drinking Acid Containing Soft Drinks

Phosphoric acid containing soft drinks, especially the brown colas, react with the metal braces and the teeth around the brackets and can produce white decalcification and discoloration of the tooth enamel around and/or under the brackets. "If it's brown, put it down," is a good memory device for children drinking colas with braces on their teeth.

Error XII—Ignoring Airway and Tongue Thrust Problems

The dentist must watch for tongue thrust as it will tend to push the upper front teeth forward so that they stick out and not overlap the lower teeth properly. Some children require a retainer with prongs on the tongue side of the teeth so as to retrain the tongue. Sometimes tongue thrust is due to an airway—nose-breathing problem and the dentist should get a consultation with an ear, nose, and throat physician. The tongue thrust problem may persist no matter what is done. It can re-open the bite and compromise the orthodontic result.

Error XIII—Failure to Cooperate with the Dentist

If your child and you do not fully cooperate with the dentist, then you cannot expect that treatment will be rapid or that the end result will be ideal or close to ideal. Cooperation means keeping appointments and seeing that elastic bands are worn when the dentist says and that the retainers are worn, etc.

CHAPTER TWENTY

THE IDEAL ORTHODONTIC RESULT

Orthodontic treatment is done for two primary reasons. The main purpose is to line up the teeth so that they meet together evenly when chewing. If the teeth are uneven, they meet at odd angles that put uneven pressure on the gums and the bones supporting the teeth. This leads to tissue and bone breakdown that is a cause of gum (periodontal) disease, the major reason for losing teeth after age 30. The second purpose is to improve the appearance of the teeth, mouth, and face. Most parents are pleased if the front teeth are pulled back into the mouth and look reasonably straight. As a result, a lot of mediocre orthodontic results are accepted. The last chapter and this chapter will give you enough information to recognize, and hopefully get, an ideal result. Inherited tooth shapes, jaw size, and face pattern sometimes prevent your dentist from getting an ideal result. The dentist should try to get as close to ideal as possible and any variations should be discussed with you prior to treatment or at least during treatment.

The ideal result does <u>not</u> have any of the 12 errors discussed in the previous chapter. No financial arch wire, flat face, gummy smile, deep bite, wisdom teeth, open spaces, rotated teeth, long front teeth, crowded teeth, uneven smile line, or discolored enamel.

The ideal orthodontic result does have:

1. Molar occlusion: The molar teeth meet evenly with each upper jaw molar fitting into the groove in the middle of the lower jaw molar and into the space in front of the lower jaw molar. Your dentist should fine-tune this occlusion by using wax sheets for the patient to chew on and to check for high spots (prematurities).

2. Teeth should fill the smile space. When a person smiles, there should be teeth from one corner of the lips to the other.

3. The upper front teeth should overlap the lower by 1-1.5 mm and rest on the wet-dry line of the lower lip when smiling.

4. The upper front teeth overjet (stick out beyond) the lower teeth by 1-1.5 mm.

5. The only gum you should see when smiling is the small triangle of gum between the teeth not a wide or deep gum line above the teeth.

6. The middle space between the teeth of the upper and lower jaw should be in line and in the middle of the face. This will be compromised if there are missing teeth. In the case of a lower missing incisor, the midline of the upper jaw may have to be centered over the center of the middle of the central incisor teeth in the lower jaw.

7. The line of the lower edges of the four upper front teeth is a flat straight line, with the cuspids (eyeteeth) slightly longer for "cuspid protected" occlusion. (When the jaw moves out to either side—the only teeth touching are the upper and lower cuspid teeth).

8. All the teeth are even and uncrowded, with no rotations.

9. The edges of the teeth should be flat to gently rounded with no sharp points. "Fang" cuspids can be rounded by the dentist.

10. Wisdom teeth out (See Chapter 23 for details). Timing of the removal of these teeth is on an <u>individual</u> basis.

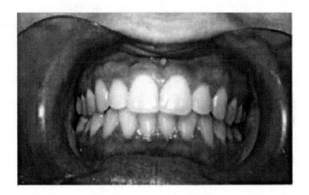

Ideal Orthodontic Result

CHAPTER TWENTY-ONE

ORTHODONTIC RELAPSE

If an orthodontic result is ideal when the treatment is finished but then changes in the next 2 to 5 years so that it is no longer an ideal result, we say that it has relapsed. From 20 percent to 40 percent of orthodontic patients show some relapse. It may be minor relapse such as a slight rotation of a cuspid (eyetooth) or slight crowding of the lower front teeth or it may be a major relapse such as a molar malocclusion or an overbite.

Relapses can be kept at about 20 percent (2 out of 10 children) by doing the things we have told you to have done: early preventive and treatment orthodontics, use of a modern technique, correction of airway problems and tongue habits, removal of the wisdom teeth when the orthodontics is finished, and using the retainers as long as the dentist directs. If these things are not done, the relapse rate will be 40 percent or over (4 out of 10 children).

No matter how skillfully the dentist does the orthodontics and how cooperative you and the child is, there will be 2 out of 10 children (20 percent) with some relapse. This does not mean that the orthodontics was wasted. It means that some part of the correction did not hold.

Relapses should be retreated as soon as possible as the longer the tooth or teeth stay in an undesirable position, the more firmly fixed in the jaw they become.

The most common relapses are in the front teeth in the lower jaw and can be corrected by sectional braces worn just on the lower teeth which make it almost invisible and therefore more acceptable for the teenager or young adult.

The most difficult major relapse is often due to a persistent tongue thrust which pushes the upper front teeth up and usually outward (open bite and overjet). This can be treated with prongs on the retainer behind the upper front teeth that will hopefully retain the tongue. This can irritate the tip of the tongue and be painful and still, occasionally, the tongue wins. Rarely does a person need to be advised to wear a retainer at night for years. This is much like an adult wearing a splint or bite plate to prevent damage from grinding the teeth in the night while asleep.

Relapse of a rotated tooth can usually be prevented by early treatment and by over correction (turning the tooth past the correct position) so that when it tries to turn back it will be in the proper position). Relapses of rotated teeth may be treated by this kind of over correction and occasionally by fibrotomy. Under a local anesthetic, some of the elastic fibers between the tooth and the gum are cut with a simple surgical procedure.

A few patients require major jaw surgery (orthognathic surgery) in order to treat relapse although this surgery is usually planned and done as part of the original orthodontic treatment. An example would be a girl whose lower jaw keeps growing in her late teen years due to an inherited family tendency.

Relapses need to be treated for the same reason the orthodontics was done in the first place; crooked teeth do not stay healthy for life. Crooked, crowded teeth develop gum disease and become loose and may need to be removed far more often than do straight, uncrowded teeth.

CHAPTER TWENTY TWO

THE STRAIGHT WIRE ORTHODONTIC TECHNIQUE

We have mentioned the Straight Wire orthodontic appliance and orthodontic system several times in our discussion of straightening teeth so you may like to have some understanding of the system and learn how it differs from older techniques and how it enables the dentist to do a superior job in shorter time.

There are two main items in orthodontic appliances: one is the arch wire that runs horizontally from one banded rear molar, across all the teeth, into a metal tube in the other molar band. There is one arch wire for the upper teeth or arch and one for the lower teeth. The other main item is the bracket which is put on each tooth so that the arch wire can be tied to every tooth. Originally, the brackets were all on metal bands that fit around each tooth in the same way that the bands on the rear molar teeth still do. About twenty-five years ago, the metal bands around the front teeth were dropped, and a small metal bracket was glued to each tooth to hold the arch wire. The metal brackets gave way to clear plastic ones and now ceramic ones are used that are about the same color as the teeth. What material the brackets are made of is not what makes the Straight Wire Technique. Brackets used in a variety of orthodontic techniques will look the same to you.

After World War II, a technique known as Edgewise became the one most used by orthodontists although the Tweed, Labial-Lingual and Begg methods were also popular. In all these techniques, much of the force that was used to try to move each tooth in the various ways it needed to go was generated by the dentist using narrow nose pliers and putting little bends and loops in the arch wire, up or down, in toward the tooth or out away from it. All this bending of the arch wire was difficult to teach and to reproduce. It was as much an art form as a science. In the 1960s, a very talented orthodontist in private practice in San Diego, Dr. Larry Andrews, grew frustrated with the limitations of the techniques used at that time and developed a system in which the force that moves the teeth was built into the base of each bracket for each tooth and did not use bends in the arch wire. He shaped the base (part glued to the tooth) of each bracket so that the slot that the arch wire fit into would be straight and level when the tooth got into the correct position. The arch wire, which has built-in springiness, may be slightly curved when it is first placed in all the brackets but it rapidly and smoothly brings the teeth into line. Instead of just being able to move the visible part of the tooth as with older techniques, the Straight Wire allows the dentist to move the root part of the teeth under the gums and avoid the gummy smile result.

Larry Andrews' technique was quickly picked up and possibly improved by Dr. Ron Roth, an orthodontist just south of San Francisco. Roth found Straight Wire so far superior to the Edgewise he had been taught that he predicted that in five years every orthodontist would be using it, but he underestimated the resistance to change within the orthodontic community, especially at our dental schools. The change he predicted has happened but it took fifteen or twenty years, not five.

Dr. Andrews, besides being an inventive genius, did not have the guild mentality so common to orthodontists at that time; he shared his knowledge with general dentists such as Dr. Walt Brehm of San Diego and Dr. William Wyatt of Hurst, Texas. These talented teachers, among others, taught Straight Wire to a whole generation of general dentists and children's dentists and effectively "deregulated" orthodontics. Dr. Andrews properly patented his new brackets as well as the little round elastic used to tie the arch wire to the bracket (previously a thin wire had to be used which jabbed the gum and often broke) and was deservedly rewarded when his "A" Company, which manufactured his items, was sold to Johnson & Johnson. Straight Wire is another example of why, as with evolutionary change, progress is often made outside of, and despite the establishment.

By far the most talented of the younger teachers of Straight Wire Orthodontics is Dr. Robert Gerety from Broken Arrow, a suburb of Tulsa, Oklahoma. Starting as a protégé of Dr. Wyatt, Gerety has become a master teacher and innovator in the field of orthodontics. He and his wife, Kay, travel the country almost full-time, giving a series of integrated courses for dentists under the auspices of the American Orthodontic Society (1-800-448-1601).

Besides teaching dentists who do full orthodontics, Dr. Gerety teaches tooth movement to dentists who do Cosmetic Dentistry for adults. These dentists can then do a better job by rotating or moving a few front teeth rather than cutting the teeth down to a nub and putting jackets on them.

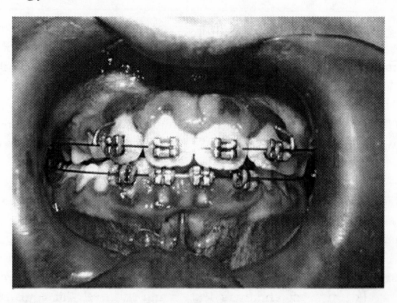

CHILD IN STRAIGHT WIRE ORTHODONTIC APPLIANCES.

CHAPTER TWENTY-THREE

WISDOM TEETH AND WHY IT IS SMART TO REMOVE THEM IN YOUR MID-TEENS

The wisdom teeth, or third molars, are thought to be disappearing, as one or more of these teeth are often missing. Our jaws are usually too short to have room for all 32 permanent teeth and as the wisdom teeth erupt 6 to 8 years after all the other teeth are in the mouth; they usually come in crooked or are blocked from coming into the mouth at all and are called impacted.

There are four main reasons why these teeth should be removed.

1. *__Crowding of the rest of the teeth.__* If allowed to erupt into the mouth, often the wisdom teeth must make room by forcing the other teeth forward and thereby crowd and jumble the front teeth. This causes a misalignment or malocclusion of the rest of the teeth which leads to stress on the jawbone surrounding the teeth. The teeth gradually loosen and are lost to "gum disease" and the patient never knows that the wisdom teeth were at fault. (Of course, this is only one of several causes and probably not the main cause of gum disease.)

2. *__Prevent relapse after orthodontic treatment__*. The last thing you need, after spending a lot of time and money on straightening your children's teeth, is for the wisdom teeth to come in and push the rest of the teeth out of line again. In almost all cases, the final part of orthodontic treatment is to remove the wisdom teeth before they erupt and make a mess of the occlusion again.

3. *__Prevent damage to and loss of the twelve-year molars__*. The teeth right in front of where the wisdom teeth try to erupt is the second permanent molars or twelve-year molars, so named as that is the average age at which they erupt. These teeth, along

115

with the first permanent molars (six-year molars) are the most important chewing teeth we have. They are also very important for an even bite (occlusion). How do wisdom teeth damage the twelve-year molars? Only too easily. As most wisdom teeth have a large crown compared to the roots and as most wisdom teeth do not have room to line up completely straight, they create a pocket in the gum between them and the second molars. That pocket causes the gum around the second molar to break down and eventually the second molar is lost and the dentist then says, "It is a good thing you have your wisdom teeth as we can use it to hang a bridge to replace this second molar I had to remove." The patient never realizes the real cause of the molar loss is the now blessed wisdom tooth. Of course, we are removing these in young people with good fluoride molars. If you are older and have heavily filled second molars that are already damaged by the wisdom teeth, you may have to try to keep them at your stage of life in order to use them for a bridge.

4. ***Prevent having to remove them as a cause of pain, numbness, infection, cysts, and tumors, later in life.*** It is a rare person who gets through life with his or her wisdom teeth intact and not causing problems listed above. The wisdom teeth, because of crowding and their location, often impact in the jawbone or under the gum and sit there hidden from view except on x-ray. "It's not hurting you so leave well enough alone," your friendly old family dentist may tell you. Of course, he will be retired or dead when your wisdom teeth cause an infection, jaw abscess or cyst or tumor; all these events can threaten your teeth and jaw as well as your life. Less than two percent of American Caucasians have both normal shaped and normal spaced wisdom teeth. A significant percentage of African-Americans do have both the jaw room and the proper shape for their third molars. Therefore, almost all white teenagers should have their wisdom teeth removed and about half the African-Americans need them out. Our experience with Oriental-Americans is limited but they seem to have the same problems with space and shape as do Caucasian Americans.

Often early in life, in one's twenties, wisdom teeth can press on the jaw nerve causing pain and/or numbness. At this stage, removal is, of course, necessary but cannot always undo the damage to the nerve and the symptoms can continue after removal. Pressure from wisdom teeth can also cause or add to problems with the jaw joints—the TMJ (temporomandibular joint) syndrome. This causes pain in the jaw joints or ears, popping noises in the jaw joints when chewing, locking jaws, and in some cases, even ringing in the ears, dizziness, and a sensation of blockage of hearing.

Removal of Wisdom Teeth

1. ___Best age for removal___ is between age 14 and 16 when the wisdom teeth rise up near the surface of the jawbone and before they develop the long roots that can press on the jaw nerve. It is so much easier on the patient and the dentist to get them out at this stage than it is 2 or 3 or 10 or 40 years later. This is for two reasons: 1) the teeth are close to the surface and do not have long, deep roots; 2) the younger the patient, the less swelling and discomfort they have. This is true for all medical and dental procedures and operations.

   Girls sometimes reach the ideal stage for wisdom teeth removal earlier than boys but there is some variation from one child to another in how early or late they are in dental maturity, which is not always exactly related to their physical maturity. The quality dentist checks on the wisdom teeth development by x-ray and keeps the parent informed and tells them when to expect the best time for removal will be and finally, lets you know when they should be removed.

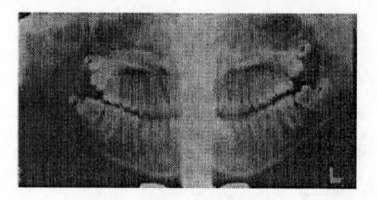

X-rays of wisdom teeth—the ones with
small ink crosses on them.

2. ***Who removes wisdom teeth?*** Most wisdom tooth removal in this country is done by oral surgeons, dentists who specialize in oral and maxillofacial surgery which covers jawbone and tooth surgery. Originally, these specialists were the only dentists trained for hospital jaw surgery but now some family dentists and children's dentists are trained in some aspects of this work and can do a good job of wisdom tooth removal. Your quality dentist should be able to tell you who are best qualified in your area.

3. ***Office or hospital?*** This mainly is a question whether the removal is to be done under a local anesthetic with a sedative or whether a full general anesthetic (completely out or asleep) is used. We do not feel comfortable about general anesthetic being used in dental offices. Although sodium pentothal is used by almost all oral surgeons in their offices, we feel that if the patient is to be put to sleep, it should be done in a hospital or hospital affiliated outpatient facility using an anesthesiologist.

It is generally safe to use a sedative such as Versed™ as a pill, injection, or in an intravenous in the office, if just enough is used to make the patient very relaxed and somewhat sleepy, but not enough to make them completely out. This sedative is then followed by an injection of local anesthetic in the jaw, in the usual way dentists do, so that the patient will not feel any discomfort while the teeth are being removed.

There are risks associated with any procedure and these should be discussed with your dental surgeon; but the risks of leaving wisdom teeth in are generally greater, in our experience, than are the problems of removing the wisdom teeth, especially if the removal is done in the mid-teens.

4. *Costs?* At the present time, the fee for removal of all four wisdom teeth is about $1,200—$1,800, up from $400 a few years ago largely due to the "lawyers tax" placed on oral surgeons by our legal system. A prominent family dentist in the Dallas suburb of Garland, Dr. Benedict Homer, is so proficient in wisdom teeth removal that he does all his teenagers in his office with a sedative and local anesthetic for about $800 for all four teeth.

SECTION IV
SOME EXTRA INFORMATION
IN BRIEF

CHAPTER TWENTY-FOUR

FOOD AND DRINK

If you have taken the fluoride supplement while pregnant and continued with the fluoride supplement for your child, her or his fluoride teeth can take a lot of abuse from a poor diet, but we are very concerned about the general health effect of the all too typical American diet—obesity, diabetes, hyperactivity alternating with sleepiness at school, soft bones (osteoporosis), etc. We offer Nutrition 101 in brief.

CANDY FOR BREAKFAST. Most children's breakfast products contain grossly excess sugar. You know them as "Frosted this" or "Honey that." (Honey is nutritionally the same simple sugar that comes out of a bag of sugar; it is refined by bees rather than at a factory). Some products advertised for children are 60% sugar! You would not feed that to your dog. Oatmeal and shredded wheat have the lowest sugar content—less than 2%. Cheerios™ are the next best with 4% sugar and have the great advantage that children like them. Read the nutrition label, add the total grams, and divide by the grams of sugar. For Cheerios™ – Fat, 2g; Total Carbohydrates, 22g, (of which 1g is Sugar); Protein, 3g. Add them and get 27g, divide by 1 and get .04, which means four parts in a hundred or 4% sugar. But look at Honey Nut Cheerios™ – Fat, 1.5g; Total Carbs, 24g (of which 11g is Sugar); Protein, 3g. Total of 28.5 divided by 11 gives .39 or 39% sugar! There is no need to do the math, just eyeball the Total Carbohydrates, and see how much of it is Sugar. Something different? Skinless, broiled chicken, straight from the fridge if need be. Or peanut butter (especially the non-homogenized type) on whole wheat bread is fine. Almost anything is better than 98% of the junk that is on the shelves of the breakfast section of the supermarket.

GREASE FOR LUNCH AT SCHOOL. School lunch programs were started in order for the government to get rid of surplus eggs, butter, cream, whole milk, lard, and red meat, most of which was piling up in overflowing storage facilities as a result of Federal Farm Subsidies. Every time school dieticians tried to lower the fat content, they were and are blocked by the Agricultural Department, which is largely controlled by various farm trade associations such as the Dairy Council, the Egg Layers of America, and the Lard Group, etc. The control is affected through Congress and some of the 70,000 lobbyists in Washington, DC and their medium of exchange is campaign contributions, or even bribes. Compounding this nutritional damage to our children is the practice of local School Boards accepting money for permitting soft drink machines in schools. If the children choose regular soft drinks they run the risk of mood swings and diabetes. Even those choosing clear caffeine and sugar free soda are risking soft bones as they tend to substitute soft drinks for the calcium rich milk they used to get at school. We should not have to tell you what to do with School Boards who are willing to damage children's health for money. The good news is that in the past year, faced with the publicity concerning childhood obesity, school boards have started to act.

WHAT CHILDREN SHOULD DRINK. Easy enough.

Good to drink:

1. Milk—generally skim milk after two years of age to avoid excess fat.

2. Water—tap or bottled

3. Natural fruit juices—100%

O.K. once or twice a week on special occasions, not as a daily routine:

1. Clear, sugar and caffeine free soft drinks

Bad to drink, should not be permitted:

1. Fruit drinks—a rip off. Tang™ has 10% juice and 90% chemical crap. Sunny Delight™ has 5% orange juice and 95% you know what. If you want juice, get 100%.

2. Sport drinks, such as Gatorade™ are for adult or child intestinal illness for fluid replacement and for grown athletes with extreme fluid loss. Sport drinks have too much sugar and salt to be a part of any child's regular diet or routine.

3. Brown colas and so-called Energy Drinks—never.

Eating Problems After 18 Months Of Age: Babies double their birth weight by six months and triple it by one year. This requires a lot of eating, but it cannot continue or they would weigh a ton by five years. Usually about 18 months, they slow down, get thinner and taller, and seem to stop eating. They also have run out of antibodies against illness that they got from the mother's blood and from nursing, and they are around more children and people. They begin to have lots of mostly respiratory illnesses. Parents or well meaning relatives can naturally assume the reason the child is getting ill so often is because they are "not eating." Some parents then try to cajole or even force the child to eat more than they want and soon we have a real feeding problem. What is the proper response?

Rule Number One: Let the child decide how much she or he eats. Force yourself not to become emotionally involved with the amount the child eats.

Rule Number Two: See that the child gets his or her basic nutrition. What is that?

1. Vitamins	• A, B, C, D—give daily multivitamin drops or a chewable pill
2. Minerals	• Fluoride drops or tablet a day • Calcium, milk, cheese, or other source • Red meat or other source of iron, or iron supplement
3. Protein	• Milk, or cheese, or chicken, or fish, or meat, or soy, etc. It can be the same thing once a day for months at a time
4. Complex (good) carbohydrates	• Cereal, brown bread, some pastas, vegetables, some fruits, etc. Can be the same one once a day for months at a time.
5. Fats	• As there are fats in all protein and many carbo foods, unless you follow too strict a low fat diet, the child will get enough.

Rule Number Three: Control sweets, sugar, and other empty calories. That can include apple juice, which of all the juices comes the closest to being an empty calorie. For rules number one and two to work you must keep the child from filling up on sweets, colas, snack foods, and all junk food and drink at meals and between meals. **The child decides how much to eat and she or he decides which of the foods that provide good nutrition he or she likes, but you, as the responsible, knowledgeable adult, determine what the child is not allowed to eat or drink.**

CHAPTER TWENTY-FIVE

PERIODONTAL DISEASE OF THE GUMS AND BONE AROUND THE TEETH

This is the disease in dentistry that will keep dentists busy in the 21st century. While many research programs are currently under way, at this time there is no known cure.

It is possible to minimize the disease process. Tartar (calcium) deposits which are secreted and deposited upon the teeth by the saliva glands must be scaled or removed off the surface of teeth both above and slightly below the gums. This material is removed by the hygienist or dentist, and, as we get older, needs attention every 3 to 6 months. Children's teeth, especially the prenatal fluoride supplemented group, seem to have a better, smoother surface, and the tartar seems to collect less on these fluoride teeth.

However, caries immune or caries free children will benefit from prophylaxis (cleaning) and a topical fluoride application which tends to reduce the gingival bacteria. The cleaning is done every six months and the fluoride treatment every six or twelve months.

Gingival Bacteria

There are "67" different varieties: including Strep, Staph, and an especially tough one which is found in mouths with active periodontal disease—*Acetiomycetes comitans*. Although toothpastes and mouth rinses have been especially developed to fight this pathogen, active antibiotic therapy along with a home care regimen is often necessary to control the process. A microscope with a video screen helps the dentist and patient to visualize what organisms they are dealing with. It is hoped that someday a vaccine will be developed against some of these germs.

Gingivitis: From plaque, lack of proper brushing after eating, hormones, vitamin deficiencies, medical diseases, medicines, lack of immune response to disease—all may be responsible for the onset. Gingivitis, which is an inflammation of the gum tissues, if not controlled, leads to periodontitis.

Periodontitis: An inflammation of the attachment membrane leading to bone loss around and between the teeth, loosening, and loss of teeth. While some patients seem to be able to tolerate a bad bite or occlusion, the most basic reason to have teeth straightened and to have a balanced occlusion is to protect against "tooth overload" and subsequent "bone overload." While periodontitis is seen in patients mostly over the age of 30 years, it can occur in teenagers.

Juvenile Periodontosis: Occurs occasionally, mostly in black male children and is a frustrating disease to try control. It attacks especially the lower front incisor and cuspid teeth. Recent research indicates that this is an immune response deficiency disease with bone loss around these teeth.

CHAPTER TWENTY-SIX

THE AMERICAN DENTAL ASSOCIATION, FLUORIDE AND TOOTH DECAY

By William D. Glenn, III, M.D.

A review of the involvement of the American Dental Association (ADA) with some of the aspects of using fluoride to reduce and eliminate tooth decay may be of interest. The ADA is a national, private organization to which 71% of the nation's dentists belong. The ADA has the most political power of any dental organization, is associated with an effective Washington lobby, and has close relations with governmental dental agencies. It also tries to project a scientific image with its small research facility in Chicago and maintains various Councils that approve or disapprove dental treatments and materials. The ADA approvals have no legal significance but do have much influence with the public, with dentists, with government agencies, and especially with the dental manufacturers such as "Uni-Proctor-Palmolive."

The first ADA pronouncement about fluoride, of which we are aware, occurred in 1937. It is worth reviewing as it illustrates the way in which the ADA operates. As you may remember, fluoride was rediscovered in the water of the Texas-Colorado area and identified in 1931 as the element responsible for the remarkable reduction of tooth decay in those areas. In 1937, Roy Cross of Kansas City, Missouri obtained a patent on a new toothpaste that contained a significant amount of sodium fluoride. The ADA's Council on Dental Therapeutics swung into action immediately. First they fed extraordinary quantities of the toothpaste to rats and were greatly disappointed when the rats thrived on it. Although they could find no problem with safety, the ADA's final conclusion was, "The use of fluoride in dentifrices is unscientific and irrational, and therefore should not be permitted." In the medical world this is known as being "quick, certain, and wrong." Why did the ADA make this ridiculous statement? Were they afraid the fluoride toothpaste would hurt their business? No, at that time there were few dentists and endless cavities. The reason was the ADA's policy that toothpaste was only a means of helping a brush to clean teeth and could not make any claims of being a treatment. The ADA decision about Cross's toothpaste had nothing to do with the question of whether his toothpaste benefited teeth or not. It was turned down because it violated ADA policy on toothpastes in general. Although the American public would have benefited from having Cross fluoride toothpaste in the 1930s rather than having to wait for Crest™ in the 1950s, we have written about this event because it is a perfect example of the way the ADA deals with scientific issues even today.

By 1942, Trendly Dean, the pioneer Public Health dentist, had established that 1.2 ppm of fluoride in the water supply would produce a 50-60 percent reduction in cavities and would not be excessive no matter how much water was drunk. In 1945, the Public Health Service began to put 1.0 ppm of fluoride into the water systems of several cities and fluoridation began. It was not until 1950, five years later that the ADA got around to giving fluoridation its official stamp of approval. Perhaps it is the function of large organizations to be five to 30 years behind the times.

Soon after fluoridation began in 1945, fluoride tablets became increasingly available nationally for children who lived in non-fluoridated areas. At that time, there was still some reason to think there was at least a partial "placental barrier" for fluoride. There was no question of safety but there may have been a genuine question of whether giving fluoride in pregnancy was beneficial. There had been one report from Dr. Dietz in St. Louis concerning the excellent results that he and Arthur W. Buehl, DDS, had obtained with prenatal fluoride tablets. (Buehl had started using fluoride tablets in 1942.) Dietz published in 1953 in the Missouri State Dental Journal and was ignored. Rueben Feltman, DDS, had published preliminary reports concerning his prenatal fluoride program in Passaic, New Jersey in 1951 and 1953, but for the 1950s, the ADA's position of being officially neutral concerning prenatal fluoride was, for once, a halfway reasonable position for that time. The ADA "neither encouraged nor discouraged prenatal fluoride for lack of information."

By 1962, the ADA officially came out against prenatal fluoride. What had happened to cause the ADA to change its opinion? The only thing that had happened was that in 1961 Feltman had published his final report of his 14-year study and found that he had achieved virtual elimination of cavities in over 350 clinic children at the Passaic Hospital by means of using prenatal and postnatal fluoride tablets. Feltman, a graduate of Penn Dental School (University of Pennsylvania), was a specialist, a Diplomate of the Board of Oral Medicine. He had a US Public Health grant that had financed his study and he used a respected biostatistician to analyze the results. His 14-year study was published in a national dental journal and therefore could not be ignored. More than a dozen companies started to add fluoride to their pregnancy vitamin-mineral capsules.

The National Institute of Dental Research (NIDR) and the ADA joined in the attack. What had Feltman done wrong? For NIDR, he had committed the unpardonable sin of finding that fluoride tablets could eliminate cavities while NIDR and the Public Health Service were bragging about a 50-60 percent reduction of cavities with fluoridated water. For the ADA, Feltman had demonstrated that prevention of dental decay would be best done by physicians prescribing fluoride pills rather than dentists treating the teeth. The ADA and NIDR orchestrated vicious attacks on Feltman and his research. They were like sharks in a feeding frenzy; Feltman and his prenatal fluoride never had a chance. Although he enjoyed a long career in dentistry, Feltman never published about fluoride again and was understandably bitter concerning the way he and his work had been treated. He had been given the Semmelweis* treatment. The

---

* Ignatz Semmelweis was the obstetrician in Vienna who demonstrated in the 1840s that childbed fever, a then usually fatal streptococcal infection in the mother after delivery, could be virtually eliminated if doctors were required to wash their hands prior to examining patients in labor, especially when coming from doing autopsies on patients who had just died of this disease. Germs were not known at that time but the concept of "contagion" was well accepted. His fellow Viennese physicians did not wish to hear that they were a large part of

attack culminated in 1966 when a group of these same ADA/NIDR dentists had themselves made into an *ad hoc* committee for the Food & Drug Administration and issued the mislabeling order that forced fluoride out of the pregnancy vitamin-mineral capsules. The excuse for this mislabeling order was that there was not sufficient proof of the beneficial effect of prenatal fluoride at that time.

A whole book could be written concerning the ADA's misdeeds but in the interest of conservation of space we will now move to the late 1970s. The senior author of this book had collected some primary (baby) teeth from patients who had prenatal fluoride (PNF) and she could see that they had a better quality enamel by just looking at them as they had an extremely dense white appearance. She thought that it would be worthwhile to subject the enamel to examinations that might give objective evidence of the difference in PNF and non-PNF enamel. Unaware, at that time, of what the ADA had done to PNF and poor Rueben Feltman, she sent coded teeth to Dr. William Lyons at the ADA research facility in Chicago. Dr. Lyons used the ADA's scanning electron microscope to examine the surface enamel of these teeth and quickly reported that there were obvious differences between the PNF and non- PNF enamel that would explain the resistance of the PNF teeth to decay. He then told us that he would do further analysis of the teeth and report to us shortly. Lyons was separated from the ADA research facility soon after and we never heard from him or those teeth again.

We actually thought the ADA would be proud of this accomplishment of its research facility. You must remember that the ADA makes a significant financial sacrifice to support their research lab so that the ADA can pretend to be a scientific organization to both the public and the Federal Trade Commission (FTC). Since the ADA research lab does not do much, they could have made good use of Lyons' findings to try to convince everyone that the ADA has the public interest at heart. Instead, the ADA decided that its need

---

the problem, and repudiated Semmelweis's experiment and proceeded to destroy him professionally and personally. It was not until much later in that century that his ideas were accepted and became known as antisepsis.

to suppress PNF was more important. The ADA only wanted to pretend Lyons' work never existed. Dr. Lyons died shortly thereafter having received no recognition for this piece of his work. We think he passed on from natural causes.

The ADA joined with the Dental Public Health Service and the National Institute of Dental Research (NIDR) to form a tag team in order to try to K.O. PNF in their 1980 symposium. The government agency, NIDR, was the major dirty tricks player at the symposium. The ADA representative was the secretary of their Council of Dental Therapeutics. These secretaries are full time employees of the ADA and are not even required to be dentists. Ours was an elderly chemist!

In 1979, when Frances's work with prenatal fluoride was picked up by the Chicago Tribune and the Knight Ridder news services and appeared in some 1500 newspapers, the inquiries the ADA received were largely handled by this chemist. The ADA's line at this time was, "Of course, this needs to be confirmed by studies by other persons." The ADA then said that Frances's was the only prenatal study. We then sent him copies of the five other highly positive prenatal fluoride tablet studies that we knew of at that time. When a *Miami Herald* science reporter called the Secretary of Therapeutics at the ADA and questioned him about other studies, he finally admitted that there had been one study done in Australia. When the ADA tries to protect or justify a policy, lying and subterfuge are considered normal means to use as it would be in any political organization. The ADA was described in the following quotation from our article in the *Journal of Dentistry for Children in September–October of 1984.*

Actually, the ADA is very much aware of the benefits of ingesting fluoride during early secretory mineralization, but believes that the organization's various vested interests require that the public not know that the "cavity prone years of childhood" can be prevented by taking a few dollars' worth of mineral supplement during pregnancy. When prevention consisted of the admonitions: "Don't eat sweets," "brush immediately after eating," and "visit your dentist twice a year," they were confident that difficulty in following the first two would force compliance with the third. When prevention threatened to become, "have your physician provide a mineral supplement during pregnancy," the ADA ceased to pretend that prevention was their primary aim and, in 1982, officially proclaimed that "solving dentists' lack of busyness was their first priority". At the same time, the ADA gave a special award to the vice president of the Coca Cola Company, presumably in appreciation for producing a beverage with sufficient phosphoric acid to dissolve almost anything.

The ADA did recognize the benefits of fluoride in toothpaste, fluoride gels for office treatment, fluoride rinses, etc. These surface treatments are of temporary benefit and therefore keep the child dependent upon the dentist for prevention of cavities and serve to perpetuate the myth that we must accept children's teeth as soft and then coat them to try to reduce their rate of decay. The companies involved with manufacturing and selling these lucrative products may repay the ADA by buying lavish advertisements in ADA publications. The ADA also charges up to $9,000 to endorse over 1,200 items. (Where is Dante when we need him?) These same companies buy off parts of the dental academic community by paying professors to write monographs that pretend to be open discussions of a subject but are actually blatant advertisements for the company's products. The monographs are then sent to all the dentists in the country as an "educational service".

What has the ADA done correctly? If the ADA's views of its members' interests happen to coincide with the public interest, the organization is actually capable of doing some good. Orthodontics is an example. Many orthodontists have tried to keep that specialty as a medieval guild and have forbidden the teaching of orthodontics to general dentists by orthodontists. No other dental specialty has behaved in this manner. Pediatric dentists and periodontists (gum specialists) have always been pathetically eager to improve general dentists' abilities in their fields. Endodontists (root canal specialists) happily share their knowledge. Only orthodontists have tried to restrict dental knowledge. They attempt to justify this action by saying they are preserving "quality" which means they want to be able to continue using obsolete techniques without being upstaged by a local family dentist or pediatric dentist straightening teeth in half the time. More importantly, by restricting the number of dentists doing orthodontics, fees can be kept high.

The orthodontists are losing this battle, in part, because the ADA will not support their effort to turn back the clock. The ADA membership is largely composed of general dentists and general dentists do not like to be told that they should not be doing any area of dental treatment that they are qualified to perform. The public benefits from this "deregulation" in the form of increased competition with reduced fees, innovative techniques, and shorter treatment times. In this case, the ADA view and the public interest coincide, so the public wins but it is not because the ADA is looking after the public interest.

Actually the ADA does what it should do and that is look after what it perceives to be the interest of its member dentists. All trades, professions, and business groups now need an organization to speak for them in Washington to give money to the lawyer-lobbyists and the lawyer-politicians who run things. We really cannot fault the ADA for not looking after public interest as they are a private organization. It is the government agency, the National Institute of Dental Research (NIDR) that is supposed to operate solely for the public good.

Are there any good dental organizations, ones that have some concern for children and the public, rather than what they think best for dentists? First on our good list would be the American Society of Dentistry for Children (ASDC). This organization was begun by general family dentists back in the 1920s in a genuine attempt to raise the level of dental care and knowledge about children's special needs. In the last 30 years, pediatric dentists have also become involved but general dentists still predominate. As they do not depend mainly upon children's cavities for their income, general dentists have been less threatened by the prospect of physicians making children's teeth almost totally immune to decay. The other reason that the ASDC attempted to follow the path of science rather than that of political self-interest is the person who was intimately involved with the organization longer than anyone, George Teuscher, D.D.S., Ph.D. Dr. Teuscher, whose remarkable academic research career began over 65 years ago, had a universally recognized superior intellect and an unquestioned integrity that was forged in an America that is as remote to our Boomers as are the Middle Ages.

Is the ADA the "worst" dental group? No, that distinction belongs, hands down, to the American Academy of Pediatric Dentistry. This small group, with the interest of about 3,000 children's dental specialists to look after, ceased even trying to pretend to have children's interest at heart in 1984. At that time, two years after the ADA survey found that dentists, by a ratio of almost 2 to 1, knew that fluoride supplements should be started in pregnancy rather than at birth, the Academy of Pediatric Dentistry was so panicked by the threat that obstetricians could prevent the cavities that most of their membership live on, they issued a new policy statement against supplying fluoride to the fetal teeth. They had the insensitivity to give, at the same time, new guidelines for sedation and anesthesia needed to repair these fluoride deficient teeth, so the members would cause less brain damage and fewer deaths among the unfortunate children whose parents followed the nutritional malpractice mandated by the Academy.

One of the Academy's leaders had, several years before, tried to get pediatricians to wait until the child was at least six months old before starting fluoride. This would guarantee even more dental repair work for Academy members. This was too much for even the ADA and NIDR, both of which repudiated this nonsense at that time.

Unfortunately for children in the US, in the late 1980s, a concerted campaign was begun in the dental literature against fluoride supplements in infants. Academic dentists from Iowa, Michigan, and North Carolina, made bold by their success in holding back prenatal fluoride, published papers and opinion pieces suggesting that the standard American Academy of Pediatrics-American Dental Association 1979 postnatal fluoride schedule should be rolled back. They took advantage of papers from a Danish dentist who, embarrassed by his country's lack of water fluoridation, was proposing that we return to the days of building soft teeth without fluoride and then using "modern" toothpaste, plastics, varnish, and fillings, and lots of time in their dental chairs in order to try to save such teeth. The prospect of more need for dental services had an obvious appeal, and those academic dentists who work for the toothpaste companies desperately wanted to deflect attention from the excess fluoride toothpaste that was being swallowed by toddlers. Under pressure from influential members, the American Dental Association (ADA), in 1993, hosted a meeting in Chicago. A large majority of those invited were the dentists who had been campaigning in the literature. Also present were Dr. Alice Horowitz from NIDR at NIH, and Dr. Herschel Horowitz, formally from NIDR, but at that meeting he was a temporary ADA consultant, and one pediatrician representative from the Academy of Pediatrics, Dr. Susan Baker, an academic pediatric gastroenterologist. The NIDR representative said she had no idea that a radical change in the schedule was to be proposed, and felt "they were blind-sided". The pediatrician said that since the 1979 schedule had cut the previous dosage in half, they should check out the problem of swallowed fluoride toothpaste in toddlers, and for making that very sensible suggestion, "I was blown out of the room". These three persons argued against the proposed change but their presence at the conference was mere window-dressing, as the outcome had been decided months before by the careful selection of the dozen other participating dentists.

The Academy of Pediatrics (AAP) was understandably reluctant to go along with this anti-nutrition, make work for dentists measure and only agreed in a temporary manner over a year later. Their excuse was that they feared the confusion that might result from having several fluoride schedules for children, as by then, Canada had three. Actually, as with American physicians in general, pediatricians only know about fluoride what dentists tell them, don't really regard teeth as a part of the child's body, at least not a part for which they are responsible, and talking to them about preventive nutrition makes their eyes glaze over. Now, thanks to the pediatricians' ignorance and cowardly abandonment of their responsibility for infant nutrition to a small group of self-serving dentists, of all people; now, for the first time in 50 years in this country, children's anterior primary teeth are officially supposed to develop with little or no fluoride, an element recognized for over 60 years as an essential ingredient of quality enamel and recognized for 35 years as an essential nutrient. Way to go, AAP! Now podiatrists can ask them to withhold calcium so they can sell leg braces and optometrists can ask that vitamin A not be supplied so they can sell glasses. Persuade the AAP that the legs and eyes are not really their responsibility and it is a slam-dunk.

I must tell you about the latest American Dental Association outrage before going to the next chapter. In 1997, the Association published a booklet for dentists to give their patients called, *Your Child's Teeth*. The booklet begins with a page titled, *Before the Baby Arrives*, which discusses pregnancy. Remember that there is no subject that dentists, by virtue of their education, training and clinical experience, are less qualified to discuss than pregnancy. Dentists know as much about the physiology of pregnancy as physicians know about teeth or about fluoride, which is very little. They manage to start out nicely, telling the reader that the baby's teeth begin to form between the third and the sixth month of pregnancy. Next, they say that a balanced diet that provides adequate amounts of vitamins A, C, and D, protein, calcium and phosphorus will provide the nutrients to develop healthy teeth. Absolutely wrong! That list will produce the soft teeth that give us the "cavity prone years of childhood." That list will produce teeth so soft that they can decay to the gum line just from nighttime breast feeding, teeth that require constant attention by the mother and the dentist.

What is wrong with the list, don't we need those things in pregnancy? Sure we do. Any fairly decent diet and a One-A-Day™ type vitamin pill will give you the three vitamins and the protein. Calcium is now recommended in pregnancy as 1,000 mg a day for women over 18 and 1,300 mg for those younger. Most women try to get 1,200-1,500 mg anyway and your physician does know calcium, so that should not be a problem. What about the last item, phosphorus? Have you ever heard of a person being deficient in phosphorus, pregnant or not? Of course not! Phosphorus is so evenly distributed across the plant and animal kingdoms that it is in anything and everything you eat. Unlike calcium which is high in some foods and low in others, there is lots of phosphorus in everything. If you eat anything at all, even a "poor" diet, you will get enough phosphorus. A pregnant women would have to starve almost to the point of death to be deficient of phosphorus.

Are there any reports in the dental or medical literature about teeth being defective for lack of phosphorus? No, there are not. Is there any evidence that extra phosphorus make teeth stronger or more healthy? No, there is not. Is there any evidence that extra calcium or extra vitamins, above the usual recommended amounts, will make the teeth stronger or healthier? Absolutely not! So why did the Dental Association make this list of nutrients and put phosphorus on it? They want you to think that they are seriously interested in you having children with strong healthy teeth and want you not to notice that they omitted any mention of the one element, the one essential nutrient that has been known for 60 years that is needed for strong healthy teeth, the one nutrient that cannot be obtained in the diet in anywhere near the 3 mg a day now recognized by the Food & Nutrition Board as the bare minimum needed in pregnancy. By now, you certainly know the name of that element!

So what would you call the people in the American Dental Association who advise parents to have defective children so their members can make their living from that defect? Snake oil salesman? Yes, in spades, but that is not strong enough. It is one thing to b.s. adults in order to sell them something, but it is quite another matter to damage children. Millions have to undergo unnecessary dental treatment and a few die, and that is more than wrong; it is evil. Dentists with a conscience should resign their membership if the ADA continues to insist that children be born with defective teeth. Parents should write their Congresspersons and Senators and ask that the presence of the ADA in government agencies be curtailed and that the **ADA be recognized for what it is, a trade union for those persons and companies who make money from a preventable birth defect.**

Regretfully, I must tell you that the nutcase Danish dentist referred to three pages ago has generated a cult (as it was so described in the December 2000 issue of the *Journal of the American Dental Association*) which has attracted some followers in some of the small countries of northern Europe which have never used water fluoridation. In 1980, the Dane, who had previously understood the effect of building fluoride into the teeth as they develop, suddenly announced his belief that it would be O.K. just to apply fluoride to the teeth after they are in the mouth. This belief was the exact opposite of the findings of all the studies and trials published in the literature for the past 65 years and were not backed up by any studies or evidence. It was strictly a belief and that is why he and his followers have been labeled a cult.

England, which boasts the worst teeth in the industrialized world, has some persons who think that one should accept the teeth that God and Nature produce and then keep a stiff upper lip so people won't notice. Some of these English, with badly capped and crooked teeth, joined the cult. A few of these came to the USA; others infiltrated from Canada and got jobs at our dental schools. Two cultists established a strong beachhead at the University of Michigan. Others are at San Francisco, Iowa, and seemingly, North Carolina. Although the cultists are relatively few in number, they have attracted a large number of fellow travelers—not because American dentists believe the nonsense they are spouting, but because they cannot resist the torrent of money that is supplied them and their dental school departments from the makers of toothpaste, sealants, varnish, rinses, gels, etc. We can hardly expect dentists to be immune to the influence of money, especially in view of the "Dotcom, Enron, WorldCom, money by any means" madness that swept the country during the last five years of the 20th century, and has continued by CEOs and Boards legally looting publicly owned companies.

Some six months after the stock market peaked, and fittingly, three weeks prior to 9/11, this foreign based cult did its best to destroy America's world-leading standard of dental prevention and to bring us down to their level; that is, to give our children English teeth. They did this through our own government's Centers of Disease Control & Prevention (CDC) in Atlanta, Georgia. The Director of the dental division of the CDC ignored competent CDC personnel and picked 24 civilian dentists of whom at least 80% were known cultists or fellow travelers. A few dentists who are knowledgable in nutritional fluoride were invited as window dressing in hopes they would make the committee seem diverse. On August 17, 2001, the committee issued a fluoride report in the name of the CDC, over the strenuous objections of our best-known fluoride persons, that were largely written to conform to the revealed beliefs of this Danish cult. The report was so bad that this country's best-known dentist fluoride expert, Dr. Hershel Howowitz, who almost single-handedly ran fluoride for NIH for some 20 years, asked that his name be removed from the report prior to publication. This was an unprecedented and brave act of conscience. Regretfully, Hersch developed a fatal illness the following year, but his career as a consultant would have been over anyway as the twenty academic dentists toothpaste salesmen who now control fluoride in the US would have punished him for his "disloyalty" by banishing him from future committees.

The CDC report of 2001 is potentially damaging to the 48 million American children between the ages of birth and 12 years as well as to the 4 million children born each year. Will the damage done us by the cultists on August 17th approach the damage done us on 9/11 by another foreign cult? Probably not, but the fact that the victims are exclusively children must be factored in.

The authors may be spoiled in that the largest part of our careers were during the golden years of fee-for-service health care when one could try one's best to help people and still do well financially. We could be described as independent political conservatives and staunch capitalists, but we have always felt that unfettered capitalism should not reign supreme in matters of health, especially the health of children. The idea of deforming children in order to sell temporary attempted remedies is totally repugnant to us, as it should be to all.

We do find it extremely unnerving that our CDC has so easily been subverted by a foreign cult at a time we must depend upon that agency as our first line of defense against bioterrorism as well as against diseases brought in accidentally by persons and goods through our porous borders.

CHAPTER TWENTY-SEVEN

ANTIFLUORIDATIONISTS

These people appeared when the government started putting fluoride into the water supply in 1945. Most antifluoridationists are semi-educated, scientifically ignorant people—the kind who believe what they read in tabloid newspapers sold in supermarkets. A few are educated and otherwise competent persons who allow their conservative political views to interfere with their scientific knowledge. Some physicians and even a few dentists have been and are antifluoridationists of this type. Others are truly deranged people who have transferred all their fears and hatreds onto fluoride and who, on this one subject, are quite insane.

Antifluoridationists try to frighten the public by describing the properties of fluorine (F^2), a gas that does not exist in nature, to fluoride (F^-), a salt that exists naturally. This is like describing the properties of chlorine (Cl^2), a gas-liquid, to chloride (Cl^-) as in sodium chloride—table salt. Obviously, the properties of chlorine, which we put in swimming pools or use to clean the patio, have nothing to do with the chloride in table salt. In the same way, the properties of the gas, fluorine, have nothing to do with the properties of fluoride as a salt, as in sodium fluoride supplements.

Their second favorite trick is to report the result of test tube use of concentrations of fluoride 1,000 or more times larger than can be reached in a human body no matter how much fluoride a person consumes. This is like putting a piece of flesh in a test tube of brine and then blaming the chloride in the brine for pickling the flesh. These people are either ignorant or crazy.

Antifluoridationists also try to frighten people by claiming that fluoride causes diseases. Actually it is the absence or <u>lack of fluoride that causes diseases</u>, the most common of which is dental decay. This occurs so commonly in children that it is thought to be a natural condition. Actually, it is due to developmental defect in the tooth enamel when the enamel has been allowed to form without being exposed to sufficient fluoride so that the enamel consists of hydroxyapatite rather than fluorapatite. The other condition that is associated with inadequate intake of fluoride is soft bones. There is strong evidence that increasing the amount of fluoride ingested, once the teeth are fully developed, can have a preventive effect on the softening of the bones, especially in women in later life. In the almost 60 years since water fluoridation started, scientists from all over the world have studied the effect of fluoridation and more importantly, they have studied populations that drink the water with 5, 10 and even 20 parts per million (ppm) fluoride in the water in areas with excess fluoride in the water. These people are ingesting 5, 10, or 20 times the fluoride in each day than they would be getting from water fluoridation. Other than the well-known effects on the teeth and the bones, there is no evidence of any harmful effect of these excessively large doses of fluoride on these adults, children, infants, or fetuses. Fluoride has been studied in the National Institute of Health by physicians to the extent that it has been determined not to be mutagenic or carcinogenic, i.e., it does not cause birth defects and does not cause malignancies. Actually, the prenatally and postnatally fluoride supplemented children are the "brightest and the best." Of course, this may be because their mothers were smart enough to take fluoride (and give fluoride) in the first place. Antifluoridationist pamphlets and propaganda should be given the same treatment we give pamphlets claiming to reveal some conspiracy by a religious or racial group. They should be thrown in the trash. If they are read, it is to remind us how many people allow their emotions to control their thoughts and actions.

The antiflouroddoppus will soon be extinct.

SECTION V

FROM PREGNANCY TO ADULTHOOD A YEAR BY YEAR GUIDE FOR THE PARENT WHAT YOU AND YOUR DENTIST SHOULD DO YEAR BY YEAR, FROM PREGNANCY THROUGH THE TEENS, FOR CHILDREN WITH PERFECT TEETH

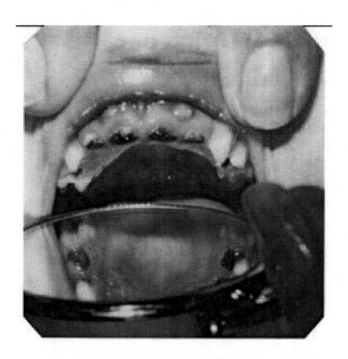

Another child whose mother failed to build fluoride into these primary (baby) teeth because she did not take fluoride supplements while pregnant. These soft teeth are called American Dental Association Teeth as they provide lots of business for its member dentists. It is no more necessary for a child to have teeth like this than it is for a child to have leg bones that bend from lack of calcium during its pregnancy.

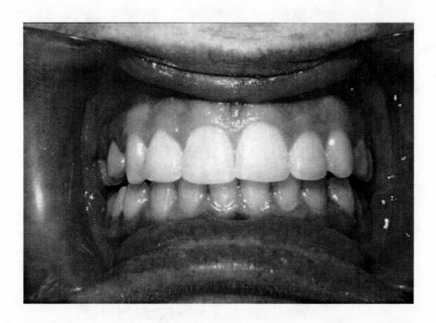

This lucky child has dense white, hard as marble teeth because his mother followed this book's fluoride supplement schedule for pregnancy and for infancy through childhood. These can be called Dr. Frances Glenn Teeth, or Children's Dental Research Society Teeth, but the best name for them is Fluoride Teeth as they contain the amount of fluoride that scientists at the National Institute of Health (NIH) found was necessary so as not to have cavities. That was in 1950!

CHAPTER TWENTY-EIGHT

PREGNANCY

General Discussion—You can do more to help your future child's teeth and general physical condition during this 9 month time than in any five years after birth. Most of the crowns of all 20 of the baby teeth and the chewing surface of the 6-year molars—the most important permanent teeth—all form and mineralize during pregnancy. Your behavior and diet will largely determine the quality of the baby and of the teeth.

Your Habits

1. *Drugs*—Stop all "recreational" drugs at least three months before you even think about getting pregnant. We deplore "adult" use of mind-altering chemicals but at least adults are doing it to themselves supposedly as a matter of choice. It is unthinkable for a mother-to-be to drug her unborn child, damage the child, and/or create a chemical dependency in that child before birth.

2. *Alcohol*—Our most extensively used drug is toxic to the brain and liver. As a result, alcoholic mothers often have brain-damaged babies (fetal alcohol syndrome). The damage that moderate drinking does is not so dramatic but it has not been demonstrated that any alcohol is safe in pregnancy. Many obstetricians permit an "occasional glass of wine" and that is certainly better than regular triple martinis, but as there is no evidence that any alcohol is completely safe for the fetus, drinking should be avoided while pregnant.

3. *Smoking*—It has been proven, in the past few years that women who smoke while pregnant have smaller babies. This is because nicotine is toxic to the metabolism as is the carbon monoxide that smokers have in their blood. Pregnancy is a good time to kick the nicotine habit that you may have started

149

in high school or college. Smaller babies are less equipped to maintain their health and prematurity is the largest cause of wastage of fetuses and babies that we have. It is tremendously costly to all when a premature baby is born.

4. *Folic Acid*—Take 400 mcg of folic acid a day before you even think of getting pregnant.

5. *Other drugs and medicines*—Do not take any medicine or drug, especially in the first three months of pregnancy unless your physician feels it is absolutely necessary. Do not take any tetracycline type antibiotics as they can cause a yellow-brown stain of the tooth enamel (includes tetracycline, Achromycin™, Terramycin™, Vibromycin™, Mystectlin™, Minocin™, etc.). Erythromycin (Zithromax, Biaxin), penicillin (ampicillin, amoxicillin), Keflex™, Ceclor™, Ceftin™, etc., are antibiotics that are safe for the teeth in pregnancy and childhood.

Your Diet—We cannot perfect teeth with calcium and fluoride alone. You need a balanced diet with protein and all the essential nutrients.

1. *Plan on a 20 to 25 pound weight gain*—mostly during the second half of the pregnancy. Moderate exercise is encouraged.

2. *Strict vegetarian diets should be relaxed* to include some milk, cheese, or eggs at least. The only children we have seen who are more sickly with even more defective teeth than those whose mothers were on a strict vegetarian diet are those on macrobiotic diets.

3. *Calcium* is needed in about the amount of 1,200 mg/day to supply the fetus and prevent leg cramps in the mother. This is the amount in a quart of skim or low fat milk or in four Tums™ tablets. It is possible that failure to drink milk during pregnancy may result in an infant with milk protein intolerance.

4. ***Iron, folic acid, and riboflavin*** are needed in increased amounts. These are supplied in the prenatal (pregnancy) vitamin-mineral capsule your physician will prescribe early in pregnancy. If you think you are pregnant and have not yet seen your doctor, take a daily multivitamin capsule.

5. ***Fluoride*** is needed starting at the 12th week in the amount of 2 mg/day (4.4 mg sodium fluoride). Two fluoride tablets, each having one mg of fluoride, should be taken together each day (or 2 tsps of fluoride rinse) on an empty stomach and not followed by a meal for 30 minutes and not by milk or calcium for at least one hour. Take your calcium and/or vitamin-mineral capsule at a different time of day. The official Food & Nutrition Board has recognized 3 mg of fluoride a day as the minimum needed in pregnancy, but the 2 mg supplement along with the little that is in your food and drink should do it.

Your Own Teeth and Gums—By now, most people know that the idea that mother loses a tooth for each child is nonsense. There are some special considerations, though, in pregnancy. You should get your teeth checked and repaired before you get pregnant. Even though most dental treatment can be done safely during pregnancy, tender pregnancy gums and concern about x-rays and medications make it smart to get your mouth shipshape before pregnancy. No x-rays, medical or dental, should be taken in the first three months of pregnancy unless there is a critical need and then a lead apron should be used over your lower abdomen.

Increases in the female hormone, estrogen, during pregnancy, often cause gum inflammation (pregnancy gingivitis). This can usually be treated by brushing with a soft toothbrush after each meal, gentle gum massaging with a finger, using a Water Pic® on a moderate setting, and rinsing with a pinch of salt and baking soda in water after each brushing using your usual fluoride toothpaste.

CHECK LIST FOR PREGNANCY

Check off each item for each pregnancy

Pregnancy Number	One	Two	Three
1. Take folic acid 400 mcg a day before and during pregnancy	( )	( )	( )
2. Stop all drugs, drinking alcohol, and smoking	( )	( )	( )
3. Balanced diet with some protein, vegetables, and fruit daily	( )	( )	( )
4. Take prenatal vitamin-mineral capsule daily	( )	( )	( )
5. Take 2 fluoride tablets (2.2 mg of fluoride and 4.4. mg of sodium fluoride) a day, on an empty stomach, not followed by a meal for 30 minutes or milk for at least one hour. Take this at a different time of day from your prenatal vitamin-mineral capsule as it usually contains calcium.	( )	( )	( )
6. Obtain 1,200 mgs of calcium a day	( )	( )	( )

Mom, when I was in your tummy, I should have opened my eyes and taken a good look around.

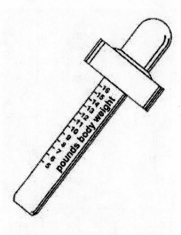

The OptiDose® Dropper

The OptiDose™ Dropper is designed to give a low daily amount of fluoride from birth to about 6 months of age in a uniquely precise fashion by adjusting the dose as the baby gains weight. As babies double their weight from birth to 6 months, if a set amount is given during that time, the baby is getting twice the fluoride per pound soon after birth than at 6 months. Although this is not a problem with the small amount given in our schedules, using OptiDose™ makes good medical and nutritional sense. The dropper is designed to fit on a standard bottle of 0.25 mg fluoride vitamin liquid, such as Tri-Vi-F1uor™ and Poly-Vi-Fluor™.

The OptiDose™ Dropper should be obtainable at http://pages. ivillage.com/raygrogan/orders/

By mail: Prophy Research, 2608 East Court St., Iowa City, IA 52245-4801.

CHAPTER TWENTY-NINE

THE INFANT FROM BIRTH TO SIX MONTHS

Originally this chapter was called "The Infant from Birth to Two Years, " but we have separated the first six months so we could emphasize the changing fluoride supplement schedule when babies are fed so many different ways and their weight is so variable.

Prior to 1979, the official amount of fluoride supplement recommended was ½ mg (0.5 mg) a day from birth to two years. We had calculated the proper amount in 1957 to be ¼ mg (0.25 mg). Since everyone had always agreed that the proper amount from age three and older was 1 mg, it is difficult to see how anyone could have thought that ½ mg (0.5 mg) was the proper amount for a seven-pound baby, but they did! As the permanent front teeth are developing from birth on, starting infants with ½ mg (0.5 mg) a day as the pediatricians had been told to do caused some white streaks in some of the children's permanent teeth. In 1979, the supplement from birth to 2 years was reduced from ½ mg (0.5 mg) to ¼ mg (0.25 mg).

What is the proper daily amount of fluoride for infants? The answer is between ⅛ mg (0.125 mg) and ¼ mg (0.25 mg). How do we know we are giving that amount? By giving a daily supplement. Since babies are so small and can drink a lot of liquids a day, we must give some thought to the amount of fluoridated water they drink. Also, one of the many benefits of prenatal fluoride supplements for the mother is that the baby's teeth have a good supply already in them and we can go quite low on the amount given for the first few months of life. If you took the prenatal fluoride, you may wait a few weeks and get the baby settled in with a feeding routine before starting the fluoride drops.

So who gets ⅛ mg and who gets ¼ mg? Basically, ⅛ mg (0.125 mg) is an extremely conservative, low dose for small babies, ones that drink fluoridated water, or if you as a parent want to risk softer teeth to avoid the possibility of a few white flecks in the teeth. The Optidose™ dropper is even more conservative as it adjusts the amount of fluoride to the baby's weight. One quarter mg (0.25 mg) is for heavy babies, or those breast fed with little or no fluoridated water drunk by the baby, or families with poor teeth, and if you, as a parent, want the strongest teeth possible and do not mind the possibility of a few white flecks, that usually only the dentist can find, in the permanent teeth.

Other facts to help in getting the proper amount of fluoride for a baby.

1. Breast milk is essentially free of fluoride.

2. Only a negligible amount of fluoride is in the liquid formulas that do not require added water and most of that fluoride is bound and not absorbed by the baby.

3. One ounce (30 ml) of "Northern" 1 ppm fluoridated tap water per pound of weight of a baby theoretically gives the baby the correct amount of fluoride.

4. Since at least 10% of the fluoride is lost prior to the water getting to your tap and if you mix it with formula, the calcium in the formula binds about 30%, you will need almost 1½ ounces of 1ppm fluoridated water per pound of the baby's weight if you want to depend on fluoridated water alone for fluoride.

5. In the Deep South, fluoridated at 0.7 ppm, you may need 2 ounces per pound of the baby's weight per day if you were to depend upon water alone for supplying fluoride.

6. If you use fluoridated water and a powdered formula, the baby will get an excess of amount of fluoride.

7. A once a day peak amount of fluoride, even a very small one, is of real benefit to the developing teeth, as compared to minute amounts 6-8 times in 24 hours.

How can we put all this together and make it simple? OK, we give all babies a daily supplement, Optidose™, or ⅛ mg (0.125 mg), or ¼ mg (0.25 mg) in the baby's mouth and restrict fluoridated tap water use so as to prevent an excess dose by using low fluoride bottled water for all or most of the infant's needs. If you took the prenatal fluoride, Optidose™ or ⅛ mg started 2-6 weeks after birth will do just fine.

Fluoride Supplement Schedule

Unlike pregnancy, where we had a lot of leeway, we must be extremely precise in the amount of fluoride we give from birth to five years; especially from birth to two years when the child is small.

If you are breast feeding:

We agree with those who promote and encourage breast-feeding, even for a short time, in order to improve the baby's immunity to disease and possibly reduce allergies. Even if a mother drinks fluoridated water and/or takes fluoride supplements, there is little or no fluoride in breast milk so you must give the baby a fluoride supplement. This is usually done using a fluoride-vitamin liquid mixture in a dropper, given right into the baby's mouth once a day. If we want to be extremely conservative we use the Optidose™, dropper on the standard 0.25 mg fluoride-vitamin liquid bottle, or the 0.125 mg (⅛ milligram) drop a day from birth to age 6 months or until the baby weighs about 15 pounds, then we use the standard amount of 0.25 mg (¼ milligram) a day until age 2. If you did not take prenatal fluoride, or if the baby is large at birth (8 pounds or over), or if terrible teeth run in either family, you can give 0.25 mg a day from birth to age 2. In all cases, limit fluoridated water in bottle supplements to less than ½ ounce (15 ml) per pound of weight per day.

If you are bottle feeding:

> ***Bottle fed—premixed formula***—no added water, fluoridated or unfluoridated area: Use the same Optidose™ or ⅛ mg (0.125 mg) or 0.25 mg (¼ mg) just as we discussed for breast fed infants.

> ***Bottle fed—concentrate***—mixed with equal amount of water. Give ⅛ mg (0.125 mg) a day into the baby and limit the use of fluoridated water to ½ ounce per pound of the baby's approximate weight per day. Use low fluoride bottled water for the rest. In low fluoride, unfluoridated areas (less than 0.5 ppm) you can use 0.25 mg (¼ mg) from birth on if the baby meets the conditions discussed on the second page of this chapter.

> ***Bottle fed—powder***—*In non-fluoridated*, low fluoride areas (less than 0.5 ppm). Use ⅛ or ¼ mg as in the discussion under breast-fed. In *fluoridated* areas, limit tap water to less than ½ ounce per pound of the baby's approximate weight, that is, if a baby weighs about 8 pounds, you do not give him over 4 ounces of fluoridated water a day; use low fluoride bottled water for the rest and give the Optidose™ supplement or the ⅛ mg (0.125 mg) drop fluoride supplement *or* you can use low fluoride bottled water for all the baby's drinking needs and give ¼ mg (0.25 mg) of fluoride supplement a day if the baby meets the requirements discussed on the second page of this chapter.

Diets

Obviously, the diet is not critical until the teeth come in, but we do not want to get the baby used to any bad habits that would damage the teeth and the child after he or she gets some teeth.

1. Do not get the baby used to a regular sweet diet. Babies do not need deserts!

2. Do not put the baby to bed with a bottle with anything in it except water.

If you have a baby from birth to six months of age, read the next chapter covering six months to two years so you will have a better understanding of what to do.

CHECKLIST FROM BIRTH TO SIX MONTHS

Baby's Name:	( )	( )	( )
1. Fluoride supplement daily Optidose™ dropper or ⅛ (0.125 mg) or ¼ (0.25 mg)	( )	( )	( )
2. Limit fluoride water to ½ ounce per pound of baby's weight per day	( )	( )	( )
3. Get baby used to healthy diet	( )	( )	( )

CHAPTER THIRTY

THE INFANT FROM SIX MONTHS TO TWO YEARS

Fluoride Supplement Schedule

Unlike pregnancy, where we had a lot of leeway, we must be extremely precise in the amount of fluoride we give from birth to five years; especially from birth to two years when the child is small.

If you are breast feeding:

We agree with those who promote and encourage breast feeding, even for a short time, in order to improve the baby's immunity to disease and possibly reduce allergies. Even if a mother drinks fluoridated water and/or takes fluoride supplements, there is little or no fluoride in breast milk so you must give the baby a fluoride supplement. This is usually done using a fluoride-vitamin liquid mixture in a dropper, given right into the baby's mouth once a day. We give 0.25 mg (one-quarter milligram) a day from age 6 months or when the baby weighs about 15 pounds to age two.

Bottle (formula) fed babies: All areas fluoridated or nonfluoridated

1. Give ¼ mg (0.25 mg) of fluoride supplement with or without baby vitamin drops into the baby's mouth daily.

2. Limit daily use of fluoridated (0.5 ppm and above) to ½ ounce per pound of weight. Use low fluoride bottled water for the rest. Do not concern yourself if your baby drinks more than that occasionally as we only need some limit on the day in and day out consumption of fluoridated water.

Your pediatrician may show you the label on the fluoride-vitamin bottle that indicates that no fluoride is needed in your fluoridated area. You remind the doctor that the label is designed for a fifty to sixty percent reduction of cavities and you wish to use the amount of fluoride required for total prevention of cavities in your children. The supplement schedule that we are giving you provides the infant and child with the optimum amount of fluoride for teeth and bones.

Formulas and Bottles

Never add sugar, honey, or syrup to the formula.

Never prop feed the baby; do not feed the infant when it is lying down—the formula can get into the back of the infant's nose through his throat and cause ear infections. Feeding lying down can cause tongue thrust.

Never enlarge opening in the nipple to speed up feeding.

Bottle with water after feeding is a good habit to get into when the baby has teeth. After feeding, whether it is by breast or bottle, give the baby a small baby bottle of water. As the baby gets older it can hold it itself. The water cleans the mouth and the additional sucking develops the cheeks and palates.

Never put the baby to bed or to nap with a bottle with anything in it except water. The combination of failure to take fluoride in pregnancy and taking a bottle of milk, formula, juice, etc. to bed causes "baby bottle syndrome" or "bottle rot," a severe form of decay that can destroy all the baby's teeth in a few months. None of our prenatal fluoride (PNF) children have had this happen, even those whose mother has violated this rule. We do not, however, want to see even our tough fluoride teeth tested in this way. The teeth will be tested by what the child eats and drinks when he or she is not under your control such as at nursery school, at the neighbors, at grandparents, etc.

Getting rid of the bottle. It is best to wean the child from the bottle by age one year. This is easy if you start at age ten to twelve months to put the things that the child likes formula, milk, apple juice, orange juice and so forth in a training cup—the kind with a lid and a spigot—or in a regular plastic cup if the child is able. Only put water in the bottle and the child will usually wean itself or will just use the bottle with water as a pacifier. Getting rid of the bottle at this age is much easier than at eighteen months or two years, and it encourages the child to become more independent and develops coordination. It also helps the teeth as the child drinks "food" liquid, such as formula, juice, etc. more quickly in a cup so there is less time for them to ferment in the mouth and produce acid which attacks the teeth.

Diet

What should your baby eat? Your child's diet will be determined by several factors such as:

1. Your family customs
2. What you think the baby should have
3. What is convenient for you to feed the child
4. The child's inborn taste preferences, if any
5. Your doctor's advice
6. Opinions of relatives, friends, books, etc.

Obviously what your child eats is personal and highly variable. If you have taken fluoride in pregnancy and given it to the child according to the schedules in this book, then diet is not as critical for the teeth as it usually is. However, there are other reasons besides the teeth for starting your child off with good nutrition. There are reasons that have to do with the health of the rest of the baby's body and with the benefits of beginning good habits to serve the child in the years ahead. Also, some of the parents reading this book did not have the opportunity to take the proper amount of fluoride in pregnancy or give it to their child as a baby and, for these children, good nutrition habits are critical for their teeth. We will therefore give you some guidelines on diet.

Sugar and sweets. Sugar is a refined carbohydrate. Simple sugar such as glucose, sucrose, corn syrup, honey, "natural sweeteners," etc., are the worst and are not needed in the diet. There is no need to give the baby desserts. The earlier you introduce the baby to sweets, the more the child wants them and the less it wants regular food. Sweets should be regarded as a treat for special occasions, not a part of the regular diet. The child's first birthday is a good time for its first taste of ice cream and child's second birthday is an excellent time for his next taste of ice cream! As the child gets older, you can make Saturday sweet day. After lunch, allow all the sweets you or the child thinks is reasonable at one sitting, then have the child brush his teeth. Even if you are strict with sugars and sweets the child will be exposed to lots of sugar as there is sugar in almost all foods; sugar is put into bread, peanut butter, canned vegetables, etc. In 1970, about 100 pounds of sugar per person was consumed in this country. By 1980, this was said to have been reduced to about 70 pounds. Most of this reduction is due to the food and beverage companies substituting corn syrup for cane and beet sugar, which is not really any nutritional improvement, but does change the statistics. We are now about to 120 pounds per person again, and as a people, fatter than ever.

Fats. Fats do not have much to do with dental health but they do have a lot to do with general health. Infants need fat in their diet because it is the only way in which they can get enough calories to fuel their rapid weight gain doubling their birth weight in six months. Some parents have been so anxious to get their baby on a low fat diet that they have caused enough malnutrition to keep their child from growing normally. Between birth and 18 months or two years, most children stop growing so rapidly and start eating much less. At this time, it is safe to start reducing the amount of fat in the diet. The "average American diet" contains far too much animal fat and saturated vegetable fat—butter, margarine, lard, fried foods, fast foods, hamburgers, hot dogs, luncheon meats, eggs, red meats, whole milk, etc. This excessive use of fats is the start of coronary artery disease and childhood is the time to start good nutritional habits.

Thumbs. The infant will discover its thumb and there is nothing you can or should do to try to prevent it. Puppies chew everything in sight and babies suck their thumbs, toes and everything in sight. From birth to two years, do not even give it a thought.

Pacifiers. These are very handy to "plug the kid in" when the infant is fussy but not hungry or when you are getting supper ready. Never coat them with anything, however.

Teeth

Rarely, babies are born with a tooth already in place. This can be a normal tooth or an extra (supernumerary) tooth. This rare condition should be checked by a children's dentist.

All of the children begin to get teeth from age 3 months to age 10 months with the average being at 6 months. Between 3 months and 6 months, most children begin to drool, bite objects in a fussy way, and may have a slight elevation of temperature at times. This usually means the first tooth will appear anywhere from a few weeks to as long as a few months. Fevers of two degrees or more (101 degrees or more rectally) are usually due to a virus or other infection. Usually all the treatment needed for teething is something cold to chew on. Freezable teething rings or donuts are sold in grocery stores. Buy two, so one can be in the freezer or ice cube part of your refrigerator and one in the baby's mouth when needed. If the gum is very swollen and the baby is really fussy, use one-half to one baby aspirin every three or four hours. Aspirin is more effective than Tylenol™ because it is an anti-inflammatory and there is inflammation in the gum or mouth around the tooth that is trying to erupt. During childhood, aspirin should not be used if the child has been exposed to influenza or chickenpox. If you or your physician prefers Tylenol™, use it instead but do not expect as much effect. Do not mix aspirin and Tylenol™ however. Use either one or the other during any one period of time. Paregoric rubbed on the gums is an old and effective remedy especially when enough is used so the child will swallow some. We do not think it is often necessary to use this opium derivative for teething. We do not use teething gels—local anesthetics.

It is almost never necessary to remove the gum above the baby tooth to help it come into the mouth. It is sometimes needed after age six for permanent teeth. Rarely, a large dark blood clot forms under the gum and the dentist can relieve this situation by opening the gum after using some local anesthetic.

The Appearance of the First Teeth

The first teeth to appear 90 percent of the time are the two lower central incisors (lower middle front teeth). It does not matter which teeth come in first. If you took the fluoride tablets in pregnancy, all the baby teeth have a nice, dense, very white look— much better than the usual, thin, pale, blue-white look of fluoride deficient baby teeth. As the infant gets old enough to appreciate praise, let the child know what lovely strong white teeth he or she has. This encourages children to take care of their mouths. Let them know that their daily fluoride tablet and a good diet are responsible for their especially white teeth (actually, it was the fluoride tablets you took when pregnant that made the baby teeth so good). The fluoride the child is now taking is for the rest of the permanent teeth. The chewing edge of the front teeth is usually uneven. This wears to a flatter line in time; do not worry about it.

Stains on Baby Teeth

Bacterial stains on the gum line (germs growing near the gum line) are not seen on fluoride teeth; but if ordinary teeth are not kept especially clean, germs growing in the plaque (white matter) near the gum line can cause greenish gum or gray black or orange stains. These must be cleaned by the dentist if you cannot clean them with a toothbrush.

Rarely, a baby tooth keeps part of the covering membrane on the tooth near the gum line and this is like the cuticle of your fingernail. The tooth cuticle called the pellicle usually wears off or is brushed off and is of no importance except that it can stain especially—usually a dark green. Again, if you cannot clean it off, let your dentist do it.

Iron Stains. Chewable iron tablets or vitamins with iron can cause a brownish stain in the chewing surfaces of the molars (back teeth). If your physician finds your child needs an iron supplement before she or he is old enough to swallow a tablet, have the doctor give your child a liquid iron supplement. You squirt a dropperful in the back of the tongue and follow with something to drink. Iron stains do not harm the teeth but can look like a cavity and are difficult to remove. Often dentists must use a diamond burr and actually remove a small amount of the tooth enamel to get the iron stain out.

Antibiotics

As in pregnancy, tetracycline type antibiotics are not to be used as they will cause a permanent yellow-gray stain on the permanent teeth that are forming under the baby teeth in the child's jaws. Do not worry about other antibiotics when medically necessary as they actually help the teeth by reducing the bacteria (germs) in the mouth that cause tooth decay when the child eats sugars and other refined foods and drinks.

Cleaning the Mouth and Teeth

Good habits should start early. Before the teeth appear, you can get the baby used to a nice clean mouth taste by following the feeding with some water to drink or by wiping the gums and/or the teeth with a small wet piece of gauze if you and the child are into that sort of thing. At about 18 months of age, the child will usually become cooperative enough to allow you to start brushing his or her teeth. Use a small brush with small even bristles such as an "Oral B™ #20" or "Butler™ children's size" or similar type brush. Do not use fluoride toothpaste until the child can rinse, spit and not swallow the toothpaste or the foam when you finish brushing. You can start brushing with only water on the brush or you can start with a non-fluoride toothpaste, which is available, such as Baby OraGel™. When the child can rinse and spit then start with a pinhead just a touch of a mild tasting fluoride toothpaste (menthol types are too strong a taste for toddlers). You brush the outside and the inside of all the teeth, especially the back molar teeth and brush the chewing surface of the back molar teeth. For small children you should just use a simple back and forth motion. There is no need to try the up and down rolling motion that we use on ourselves and older children. Be gentle with the gums. Ideally, you should brush after each feeding; however, with the new fluoride toothpaste, it is sufficient to brush after breakfast and after supper or prior to bed. When the child is old enough "to brush myself," let them. Never allow them to put the toothpaste on the brush as they will use too much. Continue to use just a touch—a small pinhead of paste. Make certain the child rinses and spits and does not swallow the toothpaste. Being careful with the amount of toothpaste and being careful that the child does not swallow the toothpaste is important because a ribbon of toothpaste the length of the bristles of the standard 1,000 ppm strength of fluoride toothpaste contains one milligram of fluoride, which is four times the proper supplement at this age. The 1,500 ppm fluoride toothpastes, such as Aim®, contain 1.5 milligrams in a bristle length ribbon which is six times the proper supplement for this age.

Trauma Prevention

The baby should learn to walk/run, if at all possible, on a carpeted floor. Shoes should be rubber soled and not slippery leather type.

Preventive Orthodontics

Do not prop feed. Do not enlarge the bottle and nipple opening. Do not worry about thumb sucking and/or pacifier use at this age; it is perfectly normal and will not do any permanent damage to the occlusion (bite). Wean by one year; encourage regular food by at least 18 months.

Interceptive Orthodontics: None at this age.

Corrective Orthodontics: None at this age.

Professional Dental Care

From birth to 2 years, infants only really need to actually be seen by a dentist if there is an obvious problem such as an unusual swelling, an extra tooth, an injury, a brown stain or black spots on the teeth, etc. Your quality dentist will provide fluoride for the baby if your physician does not. Prescribing the fluoride that this book tells you is needed should not really require formal office visits to your dentist, but if the dentist wishes to see the child, that is okay, too. Some pediatric dentists are promoting the idea of having a first visit to the dentist shortly after birth so the dentist can prescribe fluoride and advise about the use of the baby bottle. There is nothing wrong with this concept except it perpetuates the myth that preventive dental care starts at birth, when we now know that true prevention starts at the beginning of the third month of pregnancy when the teeth start to form. If the dentist wants to take total responsibility for the quality of the child's teeth, then the first visit to the dentist must be before the start of the 3rd month of pregnancy. If the dentist waits until birth, then he has missed the best chance for perfecting all the baby teeth and the chewing surface of the six-year molars. Otherwise, routine visits to the dentist for checkups, cleaning and fluoride treatments begin at age 3 to 3½ years when most children are able to cooperate.

Teething schedule

1. The four front teeth (two upper and two lower) appear between age 4 months and one year with 6 months being an average.

2. At about 18 months, the four first molars start, then cuspids (eyeteeth), and the second molars. All are usually in between age 2½ and 3.

Caution:

Be certain to keep all your fluoride tablets and drops out of reach of your children so they cannot get to them and take extra fluoride. If a child gets a few extra pills down, give a suitable punishment and forget it. If they get 10 or more or you cannot tell how many are gone, force the child to vomit right away and then have them drink lots of milk. This is usually all that is necessary but check with your physician or local emergency room, as you would if your child takes an excess of any supplement or prescribed item.

CHECKLIST FROM SIX MONTHS TO TWO YEARS

Child's Name: (   ) (   ) (   )

1. Fluoride supplement 0.25 mg
   daily   ( )   ( )   ( )

2. Limit fluoridated water to ½
   ounce per pound of body weight   ( )   ( )   ( )

3. Bottle, if used
   a) Only water at bed time
   b) No prop feeding
   c) No sugars added   ( )   ( )   ( )
   d) Weaned at one year

4. Diet control—sweets   ( )   ( )   ( )

5. Teething—teething on schedule   ( )   ( )   ( )

6. Cleaning teeth at home   ( )   ( )   ( )

7. Trauma prevention   ( )   ( )   ( )

8. Preventive orthodontics—
   Weaning at one year if bottle fed   ( )   ( )   ( )

CHAPTER THIRTY-ONE

TWO TO THREE YEARS

Fluoride

At age two we start new daily amount of fluoride supplement: ½ mg (0.5 milligram) a day. You can use drops, chewable tablets, vitamin-fluoride combinations. This is the amount for all unfluoridated and fluoridated areas (except for the few people that live in high fluoride areas with over 1.2 ppm of fluoride in the water. We can start to relax about the amount of fluoridated water drunk, but we would suggest it be limited to less than one pint a day.

Trauma

After the infant has begun to walk, this is the time when accidents can happen. A fall can injure the teeth, especially the upper from teeth that are there to eat, chew on, and preserve the space for the permanent teeth that will not appear until age six or seven. "The terrible twos" described in pediatric books can be the occasion of the child's first dental visit if he or she has not been seen in the dental office prior to that time. (It is fine to bring baby along if another child is having a dental office visit, providing that the older child is a reasonably well behaved dental patient). While one cannot totally "child proof" one's house or home, there are things to do which will help to prevent dental and other accidents.

1. Cover hard tile floors with inexpensive wall-to-wall carpeting.

2. Remove glass objects and glass tables.

3. Put out of reach all medicines, caustics (lye), and electric cords. Do not ever unplug the iron from an extension cord, with the other end still plugged into the wall—the infant can toddle or crawl along on the floor, pick up, and place the live end of the socket into its mouth, causing severe lip, palate burns to the

mouth and oral cavity. Scars may persist even with excellent plastic surgery.

4. Chairs, tables, and beds should be constructed with padded arms and backs—as infants learning to walk will bump into anything on the floor.

5. Pets should be smaller than the youngest child—they can damage the eyes and face. In short, create a safe play area and keep your eyes on your child at all times. If the mouth is bumped and swelling of the lips occurs, put a small ice cube in a baggie, and cover with a soft washcloth. Gently lift the lips to see if the teeth have been bumped, chipped, loosened, or if there are bleeding oral tissues. If so, have the dentist check this area. A dental x-ray may be needed to assess the damage. (Remember, a dental x-ray uses an infinitesimal amount of radiation—about the amount standing out in direct sunlight for five minutes). An antibiotic (non-tooth staining such as oral penicillin or erythromycin may be prescribed along with a soft diet if the teeth are slightly or moderately loose. Sometimes it is necessary to splint (wire) the tooth back into place for a few weeks). A dentist trained to work with children (a pediatric dentist) is usually better able to cope with the young child as they can be difficult management problems. Mothers may have to help hold or restrain flying hands and arms. In order to work on a two year old, a sedative may be required.

Cavities

Two-year-olds requiring teeth restored due to dental decay are difficult patients so let us hope that the fluoride supplement schedules in Chapters 27, 28, and 29 have been followed and that there is no dental decay due to the proper amount of fluoride having been built into the teeth. Continue Fluoride Supplement in the amount of 0.5 mg daily using any chewable tablet or liquid that contains no sugar. A tablet, which when chewed and swallowed, also serves as a premeasured "rinse" or topical. If any pits or cavities are found, these should be restored by the dentist because these teeth serve to chew with, keep space for the permanent teeth, and help in the articulation of speech for the next 6 to 9 years.

CHECKLIST FROM
TWO TO THREE YEARS

Child's Name:	( )	( )	( )
1. a) Fluoride supplement daily 0.5 mg b) Pint a day limit for fluoridated water	( )	( )	( )
2. Trauma prevention	( )	( )	( )
3. Diet control	( )	( )	( )
4. Teething—on schedule	( )	( )	( )
5. Preventive orthodontics a) pacifier b) airway awareness	( )	( )	( )
6. Trauma prevention	( )	( )	( )
7. Preventive orthodontics Weaning at one year, if bottle fed	( )	( )	( )

CHAPTER THIRTY-TWO

THREE TO FOUR YEARS

Fluoride

At age three, the fluoride supplement is again changed to 1 mg (one milligram) a day. This is for all areas, fluoridated or not, except for the few people who live in high natural fluoride areas with over 1.2 ppm of fluoride in the water. You can use a separate fluoride tablet or combine it with a multivitamin. As a matter of principle and of good nutrition, do not use tablets that contain sugar. It is a rare child who drinks excessive tap water at this age but up to 1 ½ pints a day would be all right.

As Gesell has noted, three becomes "the age of reason." Temper tantrums begin to subside, and many three-year-olds are ready for the outside world in the form of nursery or pre-school.

Dental checkups should consist of a panorex or panoramic x-ray that will disclose whether most of the permanent teeth are developing and whether there are extra (supernumerary) or congenitally missing permanent teeth. Also two bitewing films—small x-rays that disclose whether there is any decay between the molar teeth, where even the best trained dentists cannot see. Two small APX films of the upper and lower teeth, "close-up" picture x-rays to measure the widths and space requirements that will be needed later, should also be taken. This whole workup again uses very little x-rays if modern equipment and film are used. Cleaning of the teeth (prophylaxis) and a topical fluoride application should be done by the dentist and staff. It is wise to separate the first workup and have the cleaning and fluoride done at the second visit for several reasons. It gives the dentist an opportunity to check the youngster after a week of brushing and other hygiene instruction and the second visit "starts the actual dental treatment" and both reinforce the dental experience positively. If one has a shy child, it is easier for the child to gain confidence and respond favorably. At the first visit a check of the amount of spacing of the baby (primary) teeth is noted. If there is no extra space between front baby teeth, guidance of the wider permanent teeth by the dentist will be needed, i.e., it will be necessary to create space as each permanent tooth comes in. The bite (occlusion) should be checked. If there is a crossbite (any of the outer edge of the upper teeth somewhat INSIDE the outer edge of the lower teeth) this should be noted and a plan made to correct this as soon as the child is old enough to cooperate. Any protrusion of the upper front teeth, as well as the presence of an open bite or closed bite should be noted on the dentist's chart. Good record keeping by the dentist enables any patient to be identified easily, much as fingerprints, as no two dentitions are exactly the same.

Behavior in dental office

Generally, most three year olds are mature enough to cooperate in the dental office. Some need some premedication such as a liquid sedative an hour or so before the appointment. If the patient is handicapped in some way or unable to communicate or if the dental problems are so extensive that a general anesthetic is required, this is safely done in a hospital or outpatient setting with an MD anesthesiologist. General anesthesia for toddlers and children should not be administered in a dental office. Gas in the form of nitrous oxide (laughing gas) is not indicated in children for routine procedures and if used on a regular basis may result in liver and kidney damage and give children the idea that minor discomfort or stress is handled by getting "high."

Local anesthesia

A local anesthetic is recommended for any dental procedures that might be painful without it—the old Novocaine™ has been replaced with short, fast, deep anesthetics such as Carbocaine™. However, injecting a sedative into the gum or cheek (Nisentil™) is not safe and there have been problems and deaths, especially with young children.

Diet

Monitor the diet of your three year old. This is a time when a child may eat only one type of protein: only chicken, only cheese, etc. As long as it is protein, do not complain about lack of variety. If a child is craving sweets, it is a sure sign that the body is growing and what is needed is to INCREASE PROTEIN so that the youngster will not be hungry. At this age, they discover the fast food chains. Pizza can be a good snack food, with a glass of milk or juice. (The same calories as candy bar and soda pop and far more nutritional.) Chicken nuggets, hamburgers, hot dogs are preferable to sweets, but have excessive animal fat. Pretzels, potato chips, and crackers that do not contain sugar and additives such as artificial food dyes and preservatives are acceptable snacks. Fresh fruits, celery sticks, carrot sticks with a dip, soup, fruit, and plain cheese are excellent snacks. Any lean, sliced white meat that can be purchased and kept in the refrigerator make good sandwiches when the youngster returns from school. Again, continue the good habits begun in infancy. "Sweet time" should be once a week: a good time is Saturday morning about 10 a.m.—all the cake, candy, etc. that can be consumed in 10 minutes—then quick to the bathroom for 30 seconds of brushing and the use of the Water Pik™ (30 seconds). Three-year-olds love gadgets and their fingers can use the water-irrigating device beautifully. The devices come with separate tips for each family member and for a child should be used on a moderate speed—medium or a number range of 5-7.

Vitamin Tablet Supplement

Although it has been stated that vitamin supplements should be unnecessary if the child is eating a well balanced diet, I have not run into too many three-year-olds that actually ate such a good diet that a supplement might be unnecessary. Buy an all-purpose children's multi-vitamin that does not contain sugar or additives. There are some inexpensive ones at the grocery store; read the labels. DO NOT overdo vitamins; megadoses can be more harmful than no vitamin supplement at all. Do not use bone meal, sea kelp, or the like. These may cause harm. Some citrus, such as oranges, each day along with a glass of orange juice will provide plenty of vitamin C along with the regular children's vitamins.

Trauma

Three-year-olds generally begin to look where they are walking and have fewer accidents than two-year-olds, but they will have them on the playground. Should a tooth be knocked out of a child's mouth, and the root is whole and sound, it can be rinsed off quickly with water and repositioned back into the socket. The area is numb for a few seconds to a few minutes and the tooth can be replanted and held in place with a Kleenex™ until the child can get to the pediatric dentist's office where it can be stabilized by the dentist with some plastic mesh bonding material. Usually the "splint" stays in place for about three months until the bone around the tooth has hardened and tightened up the tooth. Again, an antibiotic should be prescribed and soft diet regimen followed. Restrict running and jumping activities. If a tooth is broken such that it cannot be smoothed off with a little sandpapering (like an emery board to a fingernail) by the dentist, the broken edge or corner may need to be bonded with a plastic material. If the break is more severe, a jacket crown (cap) may be necessary. If the nerve has been exposed by the break, some form of pulp therapy or root canal therapy may be required.

CHECKLIST FROM THREE TO FOUR YEARS

Child's Name: ( )   ( )   ( )

1. a) Fluoride supplement daily 1 mg
    b) Limit 1½ pints fluoridated water   ( )   ( )   ( )
        a day

---

2. Diet control   ( )   ( )   ( )

---

3. Brushing teeth at home   ( )   ( )   ( )

---

4. Trauma prevention house &
   playground   ( )   ( )   ( )

---

5. Dental checkup with quality dentist
   (see Chapter 9)   ( )   ( )   ( )

---

6. Panorex x-ray extra or missing teeth   ( )   ( )   ( )

---

7. Preventive orthodontics
   a) Check for cross bite   ( )   ( )   ( )
   b) Airway awareness

CHAPTER THIRTY-THREE

FOUR TO FIVE YEARS

This is a neat age group. Generally cooperative, interested, "I can do it" attitudes.

Fluoride

Continue a 1 mg fluoride tablet daily. Do NOT use gels or rinses in this age group; they are excessive and too concentrated. Emphasize a small amount of fluoride toothpaste on the brush, again so that excess unmeasured amounts of fluoride are not being ingested. The best thing about a tablet is that it is a preset, measured dose. We no longer need as much concern about how much fluoridated water is drunk—a regular pint or two are O.K.

Brush right away after meals and use a water-irrigating device Water Pik™, low or moderate speed. Flossing after the evening meal is to be encouraged. If any cavities or pits are found, these should be restored or filled. Sealants can be used but if prenatal or postnatal fluorides have been taken on a daily basis, these generally are not necessary, as the teeth are naturally sealed.

Crossbites

This is the time to correct crossbites. They are best done with the use of a fixed (cemented) appliance called a Rapid Palatal Expanding Appliance. This consists of four fitted bands with an acrylic (plastic) center which contains a key device, which when the key is turned produces pressure laterally or sideways in the upper jaw and expands both the teeth and bone. Indeed, the parent may notice spaces between the upper front baby teeth which before treatment had not had any room or space. Using this device can correct the crossbite in 10 weeks. It is advisable to leave the appliance in place for an additional two weeks to ensure stability. After the appliance is removed, the dentist should recheck in about two to four weeks to see that the result is maintaining itself. Correction allows the jaw to continue to grow properly.

A simple cuspid (eyetooth) crossbite should be corrected by the dentist reducing the edge of the involved teeth with a high-speed hand piece. After the reduction by the dentist is accomplished, a little topical fluoride is applied to the reduced surface which helps to protect that surface. Most children can have this done with a topical anesthetic while a few require local anesthesia. The mother is asked to buy the child a sugarless cold drink on the way home, give aspirin if needed, and rinse with salt water the next day.

Airway Problems. Night Grinding

If the tonsils and/or the adenoids are enlarged on a constant basis and the child's breathing is obstructed, they will snore. Often the tongue is pushed forward abnormally and protrusion of the upper teeth with a narrow mouth arch results. A dental open bite may occur and speech may be affected.

An evaluation with an ear, nose and throat physician should be made at this time. The mother should have information as to how many upper respiratory infections, sore throats, and ear problems the child has had in the past 12 months.

If the child has nasal allergies, careful use of an antihistaminic just before bedtime can be helpful. *Night Grinding* is often due to nasal allergies. Due to mouth breathing, the child's mouth gets dried out and the grinding is an attempt to moisten the mouth and feel more comfortable. Check with your physician about an antihistamine at bedtime.

Snack, But Not Junk Food

Encourage those described in previous chapters. This is a good age to chew and handle properly nuts and popcorn. Nuts are a good source of vegetable protein and any protein snacks are to be encouraged. Watch the frequency of sweets, and stick to a once a week time for treats.

CHECKLIST FROM FOUR TO FIVE YEARS

Child's Name:	( )	( )	( )
1. Fluoride supplement daily 1 mg	( )	( )	( )
2. Diet control	( )	( )	( )
3. Brushing teeth at home at least twice a day	( )	( )	( )
4. Trauma prevention playground & sports	( )	( )	( )

5. Preventive orthodontics
   a) Have dentist start to work on thumb sucking
   b) Airway evaluation by ENT if child's nose is obstructed
   c) Check for night tooth grinding
	( )	( )	( )

6. Dental checkups and cleaning with quality dentist every 6-12 months	( )	( )	( )
7. Dental fluoride treatments every 6-12 months	( )	( )	( )
8. Correct crossbites	( )	( )	( )

1965

Why, Dr. Glenn, haven't you heard about the birds & the bees?

CHAPTER THIRTY-FOUR

SIX TO EIGHT YEARS

Fluoride

Continue 1 mg a day. In unfluoridated areas with less than 1.2 ppm of fluoride in the water, you can give 2 mg a day after age 6. You can give 2 mg in fluoridated areas if the child drinks less than a pint of tap water a day on a regular basis.

Regular school is usually a smooth transition time for most youngsters. However, those with special problems and needs may illustrate behavior problems that sometimes are reflected in the dental office. The child at this age who cries easily and resists tooth brushing may be in need of some special attention.

New Teeth

Just before or after the age of six, new permanent molars come in behind the last baby molars. Often a swelling of the tissue behind the last baby molar is the first sign that a new tooth is about to appear. The child may complain about soreness and the gum may be inflamed. Again, administer the proper dose of baby or adult aspirin or Advil™/Tylenol™. Aspirin has an anti-inflammatory action that Tylenol™ does not, but if the child has the flu or has been exposed to chicken pox, Tylenol™ type products should be used.

Us first stringers are easy to spot.

Sports and Mouth Guards

As the permanent front teeth (four upper and lower) are present between six and eight years of age, the potential for breaking or fracturing these teeth is very real. If sports such as baseball, kickball, soccer, touch football are going to be played, the patient should be wearing a clear plastic mouth guard. These can be made by the dentist by taking an upper jaw mold and after plaster has been poured into the mold, a plastic form can be heated and pressed onto the plaster mold so that the mouth guard is custom fitted to the patient's teeth and arch. As the form must be dipped into boiling water for 30 seconds before it can be pressed onto the teeth, it is too hot to do this directly in the patient's mouth. There should be no strap on the mouth guard which would attach to a helmet as, especially in children this age, the strap can cause injury. An insurance policy covers mouth protectors. Do not let your child play contact sports without wearing a mouth protector. For baseball, the new plastic face covering seems to promise better protection than does the mouth guard.

Interceptive (Early) Orthodontic Treatment

If there is protrusion of the upper front teeth, such that the lips cannot close and the youngster cannot breathe properly through the nose, that is an indication for early interceptive orthodontic treatment. This can be a short phase—about six months with fixed or cemented appliances. After the teeth are positioned into good alignment, an upper retainer is worn. The lower jaw is allowed to grow forward. There may be a rest period where no braces are worn while the rest of the baby teeth are shed. If it is necessary to do a Phase II, then this may be done after most or all of the baby teeth are shed. Phase II, depending upon cooperation and Mother Nature, may take an additional 6 to 12 months. The total treatment time and expense should not be much more than if one phase of 18 months was done.

Fluoride and Vitamin Supplements and Diet

Continue a one a day vitamin supplement and a 1 or 2 mg fluoride tablet each day. Fluoride is used by the bones, especially when the child exercises, as well as being needed to continue to provide protection from tooth decay. Monitor what your child spends his allowance for—sweets and treats should be limited to once a week—all one can consume in 10 minutes. Brush and water irrigate the mouth immediately after eating, especially after sweets.

Gum Tissue

The gum tissues around the teeth should be checked by the parents once a week. An enlargement or swelling of tissues should be reported and checked by the dentist. If the child is taking any medicines: antibiotics, antihistamines, or any other medications, there often is a reaction that can be observed in the gum and mouth tissues. Prevention of gum disease begins early and it is important to keep plaque (a mixture of food, bacteria, and mucin from the saliva) from adhering to the surface of teeth.

Viruses and other medical illnesses often appear in the mouth first.

The Tongue and Mouth

The tongue should be observed for any abnormal coatings or sore spots on the tongue. Herpes I (fever blister/canker sore; old fashioned type of herpes) may occur on the tongue, lips, and the inner lining of the mouth. This is a virus that runs a course of 7-10 days. Dotting the sore spots with a Q-tip™ that has been dipped in a camphorated oil or plain Vaseline™ will often make these feel better. Rinsing with a pinch of bicarbonate of soda also will make these lesions feel better. Although some evidence has indicated that a short course of antibiotic makes these feel better and/or heal sooner, we now have specific medications for herpes infections. Acyclovir (Zovirax™), or a related medication, is used for teenagers and adults for herpes. A liquid form for children is available. It should be remembered that the use of any tetracycline systemic antibiotic (that which is swallowed) will stain permanent teeth in this age group. Erythromycin or oral penicillin can be used and these do not result in brown teeth. A recent study has shown that the use of tetracycline can be absorbed into permanent teeth in adulthood, long after the teeth have been present in the mouth.

CHECKLIST FROM SIX TO EIGHT YEARS

Child's Name: ( ) ( ) ( )

1. Fluoride supplement daily 1 or 2 mg ( ) ( ) ( )

2. Diet control ( ) ( ) ( )

3. Brushing teeth at home at least twice a day ( ) ( ) ( )

4. Trauma prevention mouth guards/face masks for baseball ( ) ( ) ( )

5. Preventive orthodontics
   a) All thumb sucking and mouth habits stopped
   b) Check airway
   c) Disk (shave) baby teeth if permanent teeth crowded or crooked ( ) ( ) ( )

6. Interceptive orthodontics
   a) Straighten buck teeth and all severe bite problems ( ) ( ) ( )

7. Dental checkups and cleaning twice a year ( ) ( ) ( )

8. Check health of gum and mouth tissues ( ) ( ) ( )

CHAPTER THIRTY-FIVE

NINE TO TWELVE YEARS

Fluorides

Continue one or two 1-mg fluoride tablets a day. Two mg is a better amount now and it does not matter how much fluoridated water the youngster drinks.

These are interesting years. The nine to eleven-year-old male may identify with the father very strongly and many mothers complain in the dental office that "this is the age of sloppiness." The youngster tries to shortcut hygiene in all forms: not taking baths, not brushing teeth, not cleaning up, and straightening his room. There is also a natural "cutting of the apron strings" with disagreeing with about everything that Mother says, the "I'll think I'll ask Dad" type syndrome. Wait it out, be patient, and at the end of this interval, the males return to mother for counsel and become, if anything, closer, usually for good.

Stand your ground about mouth hygiene: teeth must be brushed after each eating session (which may be up to six a day). Push protein in the diet as this is a time of growth.

Shedding Teeth and Space Requirements

If the dentist had to file or reduce front baby teeth in order to get the new four front upper and lower teeth in straight, this is the time that growth may occur and the amount that had been borrowed may be repaid in the form of growth in the upper and lower jaws. If the width of the dental jaws or arches has not expanded then it may be necessary to remeasure and take a set of molds or impressions and a growth plate film called a *cephalometric x-ray* and take face photographs, so that a decision can be made as to how the permanent teeth (the four cuspids, eight bicuspids, and four second

189

molars—"twelve year molars") can be placed in the mouth with no crowding and end up straight.

Dental Decay

Let us hope that there is none because prenatal and postnatal fluoride supplements were taken on a daily basis. However, if there is decay in any baby tooth that must last six months or more, it should be restored or filled. If a cavity is found in a loose baby tooth that is about to be lost or shed, the patient should go ahead and remove the baby tooth. A simple painless way is to cut a roll of gauze into a few 2" x 2" squares. Put some crushed ice into a square and hold it in contact with the loose baby tooth for several seconds. This will numb or freeze the surface so that the child can with one good tug, remove the baby tooth.

Pre-Puberty Changes

In girls, if a number of back baby teeth all seem to get loose about the same time, this is an indication that the changes of puberty are at hand. Specifically, the start of the menarche often occurs about two years after the primary molars begin to be lost. Early shedding of the baby molars or back teeth, then may indicate an earlier menarche than that seen in a slow or late shedder. Late maturers or shedders, however, can be consoled by the possibility of high intelligence. It is said that Einstein not only drove his math teacher crazy, but also sent his dentists into shock because at age 14 years, Einstein still had twelve baby teeth!

Muscle and Gum Tissue Changes

There is a mucosa covered muscle between the upper front teeth called the *frenum*. About age twelve, there should be no space between the upper two front permanent teeth. If space remains, this upper lip muscle should be checked by the dentist. Closure of the teeth can be done with braces and if the muscle is still attached in the wrong position, it may, after first closing the teeth, be repositioned surgically where it will not pull the teeth apart. There is a corresponding muscle, which is attached near the base of the lower two center teeth. If this is positioned abnormally, the tissue may be pulled away from the base of the teeth causing the gum to recede, soreness, and thus a tooth which does not have a normal gum line. A *frenectomy* (excision of the frenum) should be done. Sometimes a *gingival graft* (turning a flap of tissue over onto to the tooth to correct the soft tissue defect may be necessary. Puberty is the age when the gum begins to assume its normal adult position. There is a slight receding of the gum tissue around the permanent teeth at about 12-13 years of age which continues until mid life when the tissues appear to recede somewhat more and this process will vary in individuals depending upon the quality of the bite, and how the gum tissues are maintained.

Periodontal (Gum) Disease

The actual cause of periodontal or gum disease is not known. There are many factors that play a part including an inherited lack of immune response to the bacteria, which are always in the mouth, and the effect of a bite problem, i.e., crowded, missing, and wrongly positioned teeth. Certainly the habits of infancy and early childhood may predispose the patient to this disease which may begin about puberty in the form of gingivitis or inflamed gum tissues. Maintaining the best hygiene of the mouth will greatly curtail this disease, if not prevent it.

It is said that cavities concern us during the first 30 years; it is the second 50 years that the gums must be maintained in health if we are to keep our teeth for a lifetime. Those patients with systemic disease—juvenile diabetes, epilepsy, those who require a lot of systemic medication on a constant basis, as well as the handicapped patient, should be monitored as far as gum changes very carefully from age 9-12 years and beyond.

Injuries

As our nation continues to emphasize fitness more and more, there will be more oral or mouth injuries. The patient who participates in karate, football, soccer, baseball, and sports should be wearing mouth guards during these activities as well as other contact sports to protect the teeth. These mouth guards were described in the previous chapter. They come with an insurance policy and it cannot be emphasized how important they are to prevent broken permanent teeth, usually front ones, which are broken for life and which will require constant maintenance. No matter how good the dental bonding materials are, they still are not as good as the original natural enamel.

CHECKLIST FROM NINE TO TWELVE YEARS

Child's Name: (   )   (   )   (   )

---

1. Fluoride supplement daily, 2 mgs   ( )   ( )   ( )

---

2. Diet control   ( )   ( )   ( )

---

3. Brushing teeth at home after
   eating   ( )   ( )   ( )

---

4. Trauma prevention—sports
   guards   ( )   ( )   ( )

---

5. Orthodontics
   a) Quality dentist exam and
      discussion of any occlusion
      problems

   b) Plan and start final or full
      orthodontic treatment, if
      needed   ( )   ( )   ( )

---

6. Dental checkups and cleaning
   twice a year   ( )   ( )   ( )

---

7. Attention to health of gums   ( )   ( )   ( )

CHAPTER THIRTY-SIX

THIRTEEN TO FIFTEEN YEARS

Fluorides

Continue two 1 mg fluoride tablets a day. This is more for the bones than for the teeth as they are all already formed except for the wisdom teeth which will be removed.

Remember the "terrible twos"? Those are followed by the "Terrible or Terrific Teens."

This can be a trying age for both parents and child, but it can be weathered by communication. Communication is both talking and most importantly listening. Dentally, there is gum or gingival changes associated with the hormone changes at puberty. There is increased susceptibility to dental decay. There are infections that teenagers get which show up in the mouth—some are socially transmitted, some are not.

Ginigvitis

Determine the cause. Is it from:

- Poor hygiene: lack of brushing or improper brushing, not using water device.

- Mouth breathing: the gum tissues around the six upper and lower front teeth are inflamed, red, and may bleed.

- Medications: Acne creams for the face if applied near the mouth produce a contact-like dermatitis which resembles the mouth breathing gums.

- Any substance abuse causes a stagnant saliva and gum pathology.

Treatment for Gingivitis

Lack of early treatment for gingivitis due to ignoring the problem leads to permanent tissue changes and a nonreversible gum disease called *periodontal disease.*

Any history of anemia, especially the trait for sickle cell anemia in the black dental patient should be told to the dentist. *Juvenile periodontosis* (a progressive loss of bone and gum tissue recession) in the young male black dental patient can present a difficult condition to treat.

Poor hygiene can be corrected by the patient by carrying a fold up or pocket size brush and brushing immediately after eating. The use of a fluoride toothpaste and gel is helpful. There are also newer antibacterial pastes and rinses, along with the standbys of salt and/or baking soda rinses. (A pinch of each in a glass of cold water, rinsing several times a day.). The water irrigating device on a moderate to a higher speed as the tissues firm and heal is especially helpful. These are small and can be obtained in even smaller versions for travel.

Mouth breathing, if due to nasal allergies can be helped by taking one of the new antihistamines, such as Claritin™ or Zyrtec™. Have the dentist check the bite to see if the teenager is sleeping with his tongue between his teeth. A nighttime retainer or guard can be helpful. Of course, the tonsils and adenoids should be evaluated if they are still present and causing obstruction. Often the parent can check to see if there is snoring once the teenager has gone to sleep. If so, a consult with an ENT medical specialist is indicated.

Medications. Any external medicines for skin problems should not be placed near the mouth or lips so that while sleeping face down these are smeared onto the pillow and somehow get to the mouth tissues. Any substances being taken by the teenager whether prescribed or self-administered should be carefully evaluated and discontinued if possible.

Sometimes medications prescribed may need to be changed or modified by the physician. This is especially true in patients with chronic conditions such as epilepsy or juvenile diabetes, where the medications can cause gum tissue to enlarge or *hypertrophy*.

Antibiotics may be necessary to reduce an acute case of gingivitis. The oral penicillin group or the tetracycline group can be helpful and can be used once the twelve-year molars are in.

Regular dental care from restoring teeth to correcting any abnormal bite problems that have not already been treated is very important in this age group.

In cases where the sizes of the dental jaw is in disharmony, that is, where the lower jaw is larger than the upper, or the upper jaw may be advanced, this is the time, after growth is complete, to correct those cases that might be helped surgically where there is a real jaw size discrepancy. In the case of an underdeveloped chin, this can be made larger by an implant. The overdeveloped chin, especially in a female, can also be reduced. Sometimes the lower jaw (the mandible) needs to be advanced to make the jaws meet in proper harmony. Often the maxillo-facial surgeon (usually a dentist/oral surgeon) will team with a nose surgeon (an MD) who can reshape the nose at the same time.

Removal of the Wisdom Teeth

As with most things in life, TIMING is everything. Most of us, if we have 28 other teeth in our mouths, have no room for these last four teeth. Indeed, modern man and woman seem not to have the arch length or space to put these teeth in the mouth in a satisfactory upright condition. About age 14½ years and 15½ years (or slightly earlier for early tooth developers and maturers dentally) these teeth can be easily removed by a dental surgeon. Often there is less overall trauma if all four are removed at once. They can be removed two at a time—usually the upper and lower on the same side one week, followed by the opposite side twosome two to four weeks later. The patient should be on an appropriate antibiotic and restricted somewhat socially for a week to ten days after these removals. At this age, a prescription for control of discomfort or pain is prescribed, usually a mild analgesic tablet.

For every year that the wisdom teeth remain, there is another postoperative day of pain or trauma plus a much higher postoperative complication and infection rate. At the above age of 14-15 years, the wisdom tooth buds in the lower jaw rise to the surface of the bony ridge and can be more easily "shelled out" before they start to put roots into their jawbone. If no one is paying attention to these teeth, easily visualized on a panorex x-ray, they start to sink, put long roots on, may turn sideways and/or become totally impacted and difficult, if not almost impossible, to remove at a later date.

CHECKLIST
FROM THIRTEEN TO FIFTEEN YEARS

Child's Name: ( ) ( ) ( )

---

1. Fluoride supplement daily, 2 mgs ( ) ( ) ( )

---

2. Diet control (Good luck!) ( ) ( ) ( )

---

3. a) Brushing at home
   b) Flossing at home ( ) ( ) ( )

---

4. Trauma prevention
   a) No motorbikes or off road
      vehicles ( ) ( ) ( )
   b) Sports

---

5. Orthodontics—finishing up ( ) ( ) ( )

---

6. Get wisdom teeth out as soon as
   possible and before age 17 ( ) ( ) ( )

---

7. Dental checkups & cleaning with
   emphasis on gums twice a year ( ) ( ) ( )

CHAPTER THIRTY-SEVEN

SIXTEEN TO EIGHTEEN YEARS

The Young Adult

If we all have done our homework well (parents, teenagers, dentists, and physicians), this should be a time of satisfaction and accomplishment. These patients are about to "leave the nest" for college, job training, and to soon take their place in the real world. While the good news is that these teenagers will be independent of their parents' DAILY ADMONITIONS, they will also be on their own in many ways and this includes being responsible for their dental health. The good habits that became a part of their childhood and growing years should move forward into adulthood. The child who brushed his teeth after eating early on will continue to do the same. This group probably uses more shampoo, deodorants, toothpaste, and mouth breath fresheners than any group previously discussed. Here are some questions that have been asked by this age group.

Q. Do mouth rinses do any good for bad breath?

A. Temporary solution: good dental hygiene and not eating foods such as uncooked onions or garlic is a better solution.

Q. Does putting snuff or chewing tobacco in your cheek or mouth cause mouth cancer?

A. Yes. *DO NOT DO IT.*

Q. Do teenagers still need to take a multivitamin and fluoride tablet daily?

A. Yes. Very few teenagers eat a balanced diet and the fluoride will continue to make bones around the teeth stronger and make fluoride available to the other bones.

Q. If you are going to gargle with a mouth rinse, do you use it straight or dilute it?

A. Dilute it: follow directions on package but generally a few drops to ½ strength are desirable.

Q. What diseases are transmitted by kissing?

A. Most viral and bacterial infections can be spread or contracted orally. Disease is spread by airborne means and by water contamination as well as bodily contact. General body hygiene and health is thus very important. The sexually transmitted diseases are in a category of sufficient importance that this age group should have a discussion of these with their physician. It is important to know that hot soapy water and Clorox™ kill the AIDS virus. AIDS has not been found to be spread by mouth kissing but must be transmitted sexually, by contaminated (drug users') needles and, rarely now, by blood transfusion.

Q. Will we have to wear false teeth when we are old?

A. Many adults will never need false teeth due to cavity free teeth, a good bite (dental occlusion), and healthy gum tissues.

People who respect and care for their bodies will make regular dental visits. Those who become obese, do not exercise, smoke, take drugs, and generally neglect the health of their bodies, will have dental problems as well. Life can be difficult and short, and in a sense, our chosen job is to make the most of it—why not have the best teeth, body, and mind?

We motivate our children to accomplish their goals by being the very best examples ourselves.

CHECKLIST
FROM SIXTEEN TO EIGHTEEN YEARS

Child's Name: ( ) ( ) ( )

---

1. Fluoride supplement, 2 mgs for
   bones   ( )   ( )   ( )

---

2. No cavities or fillings   ( )   ( )   ( )

---

3. Straight, good looking teeth and
   smile   ( )   ( )   ( )

---

4. Wisdom teeth removed   ( )   ( )   ( )

---

5. Healthy gums   ( )   ( )   ( )

---

6. Continue to see dentist and
   hygienist twice a year for   ( )   ( )   ( )
   prevention of gum disease

APPENDIX I

THE REDISCOVERY OF PRENATAL FLUORIDE

Frances Glenn, growing up in Tampa Florida in the 1940s, always knew she wanted to be a dentist. Most people assumed she meant a dental hygienist. In those days the nearest dental school was Emory in Atlanta and when she interviewed there, she was told that she had absolutely marvelous credentials for admission to their school of dental hygiene, as they did not encourage women to be dentists. Frances had also applied to some northern universities and was quickly taken by the University of Pennsylvania's more prestigious dental school where, although they denied having a quota, each class of 160 students had exactly two females. After her residency at Children's Hospital in Washington, DC, she started her practice of pediatric dentistry in a small town in northwest Florida where her husband was serving as an Air Force physician. Frances found that the children were most frequently congenitally missing a different tooth from what was being taught at that time. She published her findings, which have proved correct in the ensuing 40 years.

The North Florida practice provided another opportunity for astute observation. The two nearby towns had a profound difference in their drinking water. One town had the usual river water and shallow well water of Florida with less than 0.3 parts per million (ppm) of fluoride. The other town, thanks to deep wells into an unusual rock formation, had 1.4 ppm of fluoride in its water. The children's teeth could not have been more different. Here, less than a decade after the first publications of the results of fluoridating the water of three northern cities with 1.0 ppm of fluoride, Frances could see the even greater difference with 40% more fluoride. After two years, she began a new practice in Miami which had fluoridated its water a few years before. In the next few years, she was distressed to find that the children's teeth were not becoming cavity-free, as she had seen in North Florida. While presenting a follow-up paper on her missing teeth research in order to obtain her Fellowship in the Academy of Pediatric Dentistry, she heard a presentation by Robert Boller, a dentist from the University of Minnesota, who had dissected a large number of fetal jaws and found that the baby teeth start development in the 12th week and the chewing surface of the permanent 6 year molars start the 5th month of pregnancy, all much earlier than had been previously taught. Putting this information together with what she had seen with the extra fluoride in North Florida, she prescribed a fluoride supplement for the pregnant mothers in her practice, especially those whose first child had soft teeth. Two years later, a back disorder forced Frances to take three years off from practice. When she returned, she was greeted by a happy group of mothers who could see for themselves the lovely white dense quality of these children's teeth. Frances waited until she was certain of the result, published a preliminary report in 1977, and then published the first of her nine major papers in 1979.

After 1977, Frances learned that others, mostly in Europe and Australia had found the same benefit from prenatal fluoride. One dentist in New Jersey had published his similar results from prenatal fluoride in the 1950s and, as a result, had been professionally destroyed by U.S. government health agencies. Frances was attacked by the U.S. Public Health Service for showing that water fluoridation could be improved upon by giving fluoride supplements, and by the National Institute of Dental Research (NIH) for proving their policy wrong, and by the American Dental Association for demonstrating that obstetricians could do more for dental prevention for children than could dentists. Instead of receiving accolades for demonstrating that the "cavity prone years of childhood" could be prevented by taking fluoride supplements in pregnancy, she was considered a traitor to her profession. Her husband who, as an Ear, Nose, Throat, Head, and Neck Surgeon, looks into more mouths a week than do most dentists, and could see for himself the beautiful dense white teeth Frances was producing, initially got involved in an effort to protect his wife and her cavity free children from the assaults of these powerful organizations and persons, and they have functioned as a research team ever since.

APPENDIX II

REVIEW OF PRENATAL FLUORIDE

Presented at the International Maternal Nutrition Symposium
June 11-12, 1998, Paris, France

General Background Information: Fluoride (F) was recognized as an ingredient of fossilized tusks and teeth of mastadons in Italy in 1805. F, as KF and CaF$_2$, was utilized as a systemic nutrient for the benefit of teeth in France, Germany, and England in the mid-1800s. It was forgotten and rediscovered in excessive amounts in the water of a few volcanic areas in 1931. Dean found that children in areas with 1.2 parts per million (ppm) of F in the water had a 50%-60% reduction in caries with no objectionable tooth staining (*Pub Health Rep 53:1443-52, 1939; 56:761- 92, 1941; 57:1155-79, 1942*). Water fluoridation, at 1.0 ppm, began in the USA in 1945 and now involves almost 60% of the population. In France, salt fluoridation serves a similar purpose. The advantage of fluoridation, water or salt, is that some F benefit is provided for most everyone as a public health measure. The disadvantage is that almost no one receives a precise daily optimum amount of F and almost none is supplied to the primary teeth and the first permanent molars, which undergo a critical phase of their mineralization during pregnancy. F tablet supplementation, starting the third month of pregnancy will perfect those teeth for the informed and compliant, without interfering with the general benefit of water or salt fluoridation.

Children who live in areas with over 1.5-2.0 ppm of natural F in their water will often have undesirable staining of their permanent teeth, except for their first permanent molars. The anterior primary teeth, which develop almost entirely in pregnancy, do not stain from excessive F until the concentration reaches 8-12 ppm with an assumed dose of 8-12 mg/day for the pregnant women (Smith et al., *JADA* 22:814-17, 1935). This finding gave rise to the concept of a placental barrier for F. In 1962 at the Karolinska, Ericsson found immediate placental passage, but with the fetus having less than 1/4 the peak serum value of the mother (*Acta Obstet Gyne Scan* 31:144-58, 1962). This disparity is due to the rapid maternal renal excretion and uptake in the large mass of material bones, and is called the maternal loss of F (Glenn et al., *J Dent Child* 54:445-50, 1987; Gedalia et al., *Adv Dent Res* 3(2):168-176, 1989). The maternal loss of F explains why the primary teeth and first permanent molars are so much softer and more prone to decay than are the rest of the permanent teeth that develop entirely postnatally. Placental F passage has been confirmed in Paris (Caldara, Chavinie et al., *Biol Neonate 54:263-9, 1988).*

In the USA, some of the early research done with F supplements was by persons who seemed to function as antifluoridationists as they showed that precise F supplements were of more benefit to the individual than was fluoridated water. Supplements were then seen as a threat to the cause of fluoridation and attacked by Public Health dentists. In 1966, when sales of the twelve different brands of prenatal vitamin-fluoride capsules greatly increased, National Institute of Dental Research (NIDR, NIH) personnel and American Dental Association (ADA) persons, acting as a Food and Drug Administration (FDA) ad hoc committee made illegal, not the prescribing of F in pregnancy, but the labeling and promotion of F in prenatal vitamin capsules. This caused them to stop being manufactured. When a physician in Wisconsin attempted to keep people from voting for fluoridation by saying that it would harm the fetus, the Public Health dentists exaggerated the "placental barrier" and said that F could not cause harm because it did not cross the placenta. As the evidence accumulated that F, as a small water borne electrolyte, easily crossed the placenta and caused obvious benefit to the teeth, the dentists were hoist by their own petard. Thus, in the USA, the original opposition to prenatal fluoride supplements (PNF) arose from the politics of fluoridation. Later, when F topicals, toothpaste, rinses, and gels became so profitable, opposition came from those who required F deficient teeth that greatly need such items. Most recently, as too many dentists compete for fewer cavities in the USA, dental organizations have made it clear that while they are willing to support fluoridation to give their dentist members a better quality of enamel in which to place restorations, they want nothing to do with any program that puts virtual total elimination of cavities into the hands of physicians. The ADA was officially neutral on the subject in the 1950s, but went negative as the positive studies were published in the 1960s. The motivation of these persons has been politics and money, not science, and their method has been to deny the validity on the studies showing benefit from PNF. We should, therefore, review that evidence ourselves.

Prenatal water fluoridation studies: Three of the classic water fluoridation studies in the USA examined the question whether exposure to F water during pregnancy gave additional benefit to the resultant children's teeth as compared to exposure to F water starting at birth. *(Arnold, Dean, Jay et al, Pub Health Rep 71:652-58, 1956; Blaney & Hill, JADA 69:291-4, 1964; Tank & Storvick, JADA 69:749-57, 1964)* Also, there was a large 10-year study in Philadelphia *(Soricelli et al., Penn Dent J 32:47-51, 1964)*, a NIDR study in Minneapolis *(Horowitz et al., Pub Health Rep 82:297-304, 1967)*, and one in Canada *(Lewis et al., J Canad Dent Assoc., 4:14044, 1972)*. These six studies all found additional reduction in dental caries in the primary teeth due to exposure to F water during pregnancy, ranging from 10% to 35%. In addition, Horowitz found 18% less caries in the first permanent molars, at just age seven years, from the prenatal exposure. There is one small study, with less than 60 children per cohort, which failed to find any additional benefit. *(Carlos et al., Pub Health Rep 77:658- 60, 1962)* Carlos was one of the persons at NIDR responsible for the 1966 ban on PNF labeling. The reports of Lemke and Grainger do not address the question and the report of Katz et al. has such obvious internal contradictions with its data that everyone, including Stamm, feels it should be disregarded. It should be mentioned that Horowitz's Minneapolis study is almost always incorrectly characterized in review papers. There were groups of about 500 children with different amounts of exposure during pregnancy and at birth. Incisors were omitted. Comparing the two groups with little or no exposure to F water during gestation with the two groups with 6-9 months exposure, there was an additional 10% reduction in caries in the primary cupids and molars and an 18% reduction in the first permanent molars. He termed this "a slight downward trend" and concluded that it was not significant. It is this conclusion that review authors quote even though the data are quite positive. He denigrated his own findings because the agency, for which he worked, NIDR, had in 1966, taken the labeling action described previously. In summary: six studies, five are large, three are classics, all show benefit from prenatal fluoridated water, versus one small negative study.

Prenatal fluoride tablet supplementation (PNF) studies: PNF provides the maternal peak serum levels for about 30 minutes once a day that are necessary to get meaningful amounts of F past the maternal loss of F (formally known as the placental barrier) and into the mineralizing fetal teeth. There are seven large trials and three smaller reports, and all are positive ranging from 10% (45% initially) less caries for Leverett, & 30-99% for the rest. Most used 1 mg F/day (2.2 mg NaF), Light used 1.5 mg, and Glenn used 2 mg—1 mg via F water and a 1 mg F supplement, increasing the supplement to 2 mg in 1987. The seven are: *(Feltman et al., J DentMed 16:190-98, 1961; Pritchard, Aust Dent J 14:335-8, 1967; Kadis et al., Med J Aust 2:103 7-40, 1968; Hoskova, Cesk Pediatr 23:438-41, 1968; Schutzmannsky, Disch Stomatol 21:122-9, 1971; Glenn et al., J Dent Child 44:391-4, 1977; 46:17-21, 1979; 48:18-22, 1981; 51:19-23, 1984; 51:344-51, 1984; 54:445- 50,1987; 67:317-21,1997, Am J Obstet Gyne 143: 560- 64,1982; LeGeros, Glenn et al, J Dent Res 64:465-9, 1985; Leverett et al., J Dent Res 71:1224, 1992; Final Report: 7- 54, MDR, NIH, Washington, DC; Caries Res 31:174-9, 1997.* The three smaller reports are: *(Dietz, J MO State Dent Assoc 33:12-4, 1953; Light et al., JADA 56:249-50, 1958; Light, Bibby et al., J Dent Res 47:668, 1968).* As with Horowitz's NIDR F water study, the results of Leverett's NIDR tablet study are being misstated. In 1992, Leverett reported that the results of decayed filled surfaces (dfs) for the controls were 0.55 and were 0.30 for the PNFs, a 45% reduction in decay. When published in *Caries Research* after his death five years later, the figures were changed to 0.50 and 0.45, a 10% reduction in decay. The PNFs had gained 50% more cavities while the controls lost 10 % of theirs! This publication also withheld that fact that the PNFs had a 16% reduction in prematurity, a slightly higher birth weight, and that

16% more control children had cavities than did the PNFs. *Caries Research*, which seems to function as an in-house advertising organ for Unilever, has a long standing policy of not permitting letters to the editor. In view of this journal's self-interested prejudice against nutritional fluoride, and considering the abysmal incompetence of the editing, this seems a prudent policy indeed. In summary: ten PNF tablet studies—all positive. Leverett reported 96% of the PNF children cavity free at age 3 years and 92.5 % free at age 5 years; Glenn found 97% cavity free at 5 years, and when followed by postnatal F supplements, 93% never having had a cavity at age 17, compared to the national average of 16% cavity free at that age. In Milan, Brambilla recently found that 1 mg F is only at the threshold of the amount that a pregnant woman must ingest at one time in order for the F to be expressed in the fetus and supported the larger daily dose of Glenn et al. *(Archs oral Biol 39:991-4, 1994).*

Ancillary evidence for the efficacy of PNF: The entire literature that demonstrates the preeruptive benefit of nutritional F, started from birth, for the permanent teeth which erupt 6-12 years later, is pertinent. Two reviews of this data are: *(Marthaler, in Continuing Evaluation of the Use of Fluorides. Washington, Amer. Assoc. Adv. Science, 1979; Murray, Rugg-Gunn, Jenkins, in Fluorides in Caries Prevention. London, Butterworth Heinemann, 1991)* PNF is simply preeruptive nutritional F for the primary teeth and the occlusal (chewing surface) of the first permanent molars. The study by Aasenden & Peebles, a Norwegian female dentist and an American male pediatrician, produced the best two papers ever written about nutritional F. The papers tell us all we need know about systemic F, including, by obvious inference, the need for PNF. The only teeth that they failed to protect from caries with high dose postnatal F supplements were those teeth that begin their development during pregnancy. *(Aasenden and Peebles, Archs oral Biol 19:321-6, 1974; 23:111-5, 1978).* In Holland, the teeth least benefited by water fluoridation were recognized as "the ones formed and partly calcified in a period of small F uptake by the fetus and young child (pregnancy and lactation)." *(Baker Dirks et al., Archs oral Biol 4(s.i) 187-92, 1961).*

Evidence from the examination of PNF and non-PNF teeth: It has been long recognized that molars that develop with F have smoother occlusal surfaces that make them less susceptible to decay. PNF teeth have this characteristic. *(Glenn et al., J Dent Child 51:19-23, 1984).* It has been long known that caries resistant teeth have high levels of F in their enamel. PNF teeth have about three times the amount as compared to teeth with only F water and five times the amount compared to teeth produced without any extra F. *(Glenn et al., J Dent Child 51:344-51, 1984; LeGeros, Glenn, et al., J Dent Res 64:465-9, 1985).* LeGeros found that the PNF enamel had the tight crystallinity that had been formally thought to be only found in permanent tooth enamel. In Germany, it was found that PNF expressed itself by doubling the amount of F in the postnatally formed enamel despite all children having extremely high dose postnatal F supplements from birth. *(Kunzel et al., Zahn-, Mund-Kieferheild 73:3-9, 1985)* The results are available in English in: *(Gedalia et al., Adv Dent Res 3(2): 168-76, 1989; Glenn et al., J Dent Child 67:317-21, 1997).*

Evidence of "medical" benefits from PNF—birth statistics, growth and development: In 1976, low birth weight was found associated with lower F tissue levels. *(Hellstrom, Scan J Dent Res 84:119-36, 1976.)* Glenn et al. found PNF associated with reduced prematurity and higher birth weight. *(Am J Obstet Gyne 143: 560-4, 1982).* The Harvard School of Public Health found improved pregnancy outcomes with increased F in the water. *(Aschengrau et al., Arch Environ Health 48:105-13, 1993).* Leverett reported a 16% reduction in prematurity and a slightly higher birth weight with even just 1 mg PNF/day. *(Leverett, Final Report 7183-6191: 1-54, NIDR-NIH, Bethesda, MD, 1992).* The World Health Organization reported that PNF infants gain more weight their first year of life and called for more PNF studies *(Trace Elements in Human Nutrition and Health, WHO, Geneva, 1996, p. 118).* For more on "medical" benefits, see *Glenn et al. J Dent Child 67:317-21, 1997.*

Latest development: The Food and Nutrition Board of the National Academy of Sciences, the quasi-governmental group of academic nutritionists who set the official USA standards, has just recognized 3 mg of F/day in pregnancy as the minimum Adequate Intake (AI) with a Upper Limit of 10 mg. They did not yet recommend supplementation, but as most F in foods is bound and not bioavailable, and as F is bioavailable in water and water based beverages, in swallowed F toothpaste (significant only in young children), and as a NaF supplement, the only way this nutritional goal can be met in virtually all women, is by a NaF supplement. Even in fluoridated communities, adult total daily fluoride intake has been found to be only 0.4—2.4 mg *(Dietary Reference Intakes for Ca, P, Mg, Vit. D, and F. Washington, DC, National Academy Press, 1997).*

PNF Summary: The evidence that prenatal fluoride supplementation prevents the most common birth defect in the world, the soft fluoride deficient teeth hidden beneath the baby's gums, is overwhelming and evident to anyone who does not earn his living from the care of children's teeth. *(Glenn, La Prevention Bucco-Dentaire 13:27-8, 1983)* The evidence that there are general medical birth and growth and development benefits is intriguing and consistent with what is known about other essential trace nutrients, but is not yet completely proven. Health professionals should inform their patients about PNF and encourage their pregnant patients to take a 2 mg F supplement (4.4 mg NaF) a day on an empty stomach, not followed by food or milk for 30 minutes, and at a different time from her vitamin-mineral pregnancy capsule. The cost is minimal and it will also be of help for osteoporosis prevention in the mother. We have been doing this preventive nutrition for thousands of persons for over 35 years, in many cases for two generations in the same family, and for the last grandchild of (former) President George H.W. Bush, and have never had a complaint about the appearance or quality of the resultant teeth or child.

Children's Dental Research Society
PO Box 64-3219
Vero Beach, FL 32964
E-mail: childrenwithperfectteeth.com

APPENDIX III

Dr. Frances Glenn's ten published papers on fluoride; she has published seven papers on other dental topics.

1. Immunity Conveyed by Fluoride Supplement During Pregnancy. *Journal Dentistry Children, 1977.*

2. *Immunity Conveyed by Fluoride Supplement During Pregnancy. Part II. Journal Dentistry Children, 1979.*

3. *The rationale for the Administration of a NaF tablet supplement during pregnancy and postnatally in a Private Practice Setting. Part III. Journal Dentistry Children, 1981.*

4. *Fluoride Tablet Supplementation during Pregnancy for Caries Immunity: a study of the Offspring Produced. Part IV. American Journal of Obstetrics and Gynecology, 1982.*

5. *Enfants Sans Carie, La Prevention Bucco-Dentaire 13: 27-8, 1983 [Part VIII]*

6. *Prenatal Fluoride Supplementation and Improved Molar Morphology. Part V. Journal Dentistry Children, 1984.*

7. *Prenatal Fluoride Tablet Supplementation and the Fluoride Content of Teeth. Part VII. Journal Dentistry Children, 1984.*

8. *Comparative Physicochemical Properties of Deciduous Enamel with and without prenatal fluoride tablet supplementation. (PNF). Part VI. Journal Dental Research, 1985.*

9. *Optimum Dosage for Prenatal Fluoride Supplementation. Part IX, Journal Dentistry Children, 1987.*

10. *Prenatal Fluoride for Growth and Development: Part X. Journal Dentistry Children*, 1997.

INDEX

ABOUT THE AUTHOR

Dr. Frances Glenn has 45 years experience as a Pediatric Dentist and is certified in Orthodontics. She enjoys an international reputation in the fields of congenitally missing teeth, using fluoride nutrition to build teeth that do not have cavities, and in identifying a fungus causing gum infections in young children. She has the largest and longest followed series of cavity-free children in the dental literature, and her publications are cited in more than 15 major medical and dental textbooks. She has lectured all over the world and has gained many honors, including being the first woman dentist to receive the Outstanding Alumni Award from the University of Pennsylvania Dental School and has served on the Board of Overseers at that school for the past 17 years. Her physician husband has assisted in her research and writings for the last 20 years.

"I agree with and support Dr. Glenn's findings and her program."

Dr. Itzak Gedalia, Ph.D, Professor, Hadassah Dental School. Israel's & Europe's most accomplished person in dental research.

"I prescribed Dr. Glenn's recommendations for my patients."

Dr. Charles Kalstone, M.D. Named "Miami's Obstetrician To The Stars"

"Dr. Glenn's book should be read by everyone concerned with children's health."

Dr. Herbert Scharpf, D.M.D. Captain, US Navy Dental Corp (Ret.) Former Chief of Oral & Maxillofacial Surgery, US Navy Hospital, San Diego

"This book offers abundant information concerning dental health that is not generally available to the public, and 'tells it like it is' ".

Dr. Benedict Homer, D.D.S., Dallas, Texas; Past President, American Orthodontic Society

Printed in the United States
82705LV00004B/61-63/A